The
MENSA
Think-Smart Book

By Dr. Abbie F. Salny
and Lewis Burke Frumkes

PERENNIAL LIBRARY

HARPER & ROW, PUBLISHERS
New York, Cambridge, Philadelphia, San Francisco
London, Mexico City, São Paulo, Singapore, Sydney

To Marvin, who always thought smart

For Jerry
—A.S.
For Timothy and Amber
—L.B.F.

THE MENSA THINK-SMART BOOK. Copyright © 1986 by Abbie F. Salny and Lewis Burke Frumkes. All rights reserved. Printed in the United States of America. No part of this book may be used or reproduced in any manner whatsoever without written permission except in the case of brief quotations embodied in critical articles and reviews. For information address Harper & Row, Publishers, Inc., 10 East 53rd Street, New York, N.Y. 10022. Published simultaneously in Canada by Fitzhenry & Whiteside Limited, Toronto.

FIRST EDITION

Designer: C. Linda Dingler

Library of Congress Cataloging-in-Publication Data

Salny, Abbie F.
   The Mensa think-smart book.

   "Perennial Library."
   1. Intellect—Problems, exercises, etc.   2. Puzzles.
3. Questions and answers.   4. Mensa.   I. Frumkes, Lewis Burke.
II. Title.
BF431.3.S25   1986   153   84-48619
ISBN 0-06-091255-3 (pbk.)

89 90 MPC 10

CONTENTS

ABOUT THE AUTHORS

Psychologist Dr. Abbie F. Salny is the co-author of the best-selling *Mensa Genius Quiz Books* (over 100,000 copies in print) and of the new Harper & Row paperback *The True Cognoscente's Culture Test.*

Lewis Burke Frumkes, the author of *How to Raise Your IQ by Eating Gifted Children,* is the former humor editor of the *Mensa Bulletin.*

1

INTRODUCTION:
THINKING SMART

When Karl Friedrich Gauss, the great mathematician, was ten years old, the members of his school class were asked to cast up the sum of all the numbers between one and a hundred. While the other students toiled over this seemingly laborious problem, Gauss raised his hand within seconds and gave the answer five thousand and fifty. "That's correct!" exclaimed the teacher. "How in the world did you get the answer so quickly?" The precocious youth replied: "It was really quite simple. There are forty-nine pairs of numbers between one and one hundred that add up to one hundred: ninety-nine and one, ninety-eight and two, ninety-seven and three, etc. That makes forty-nine hundred, then I added one hundred because it stands alone, and fifty which stands alone in the center. Together this makes five thousand and fifty."

We do not pretend that in *The Mensa Think-Smart Book* we can transform you into a Gauss or an Einstein who can make conceptual leaps of this magnitude (at least not immediately), but we can promise that if you read our chapters carefully and do all the exercises and quizzes, as outlined, you will discover such words as "hirple," "adscititious," and "feeze," which you probably never knew existed; improve your memory so that you can recite a list of twenty objects backward after having heard them only once; and understand, at last, the difference between a code and a cipher, so that you will no longer have to drag along your Rosetta stone to parties. There is also a good likelihood that you will begin to think more like Mensans think—quick and sharp—become productive intellectually, if you aren't already, and, for sure, have a barrel of fun in the process.

In *The Mensa Think-Smart Book* the authors are not primarily concerned with elevating an abstract IQ test result—though this might in fact occur—but rather with teaching you little aids, tricks, and shortcuts with which to battle the morass of facts and figures that daily oppress our lives. In this age of media hype, computer printouts, and junk mail, we can all use help in solving problems easily so as to free up valuable time. *The Mensa Think-Smart Book* will provide that help.

For those aspiring logicians out there, *The Mensa Think-Smart Book* will teach the popular types of logic puzzles and how to solve them. Remember the old truthteller/liar stories, and gallon-can problems, that used to tie you in knots and keep you up all night? Or the ones about the black spots and the white spots, and ferrying chickens across the river? Rest easy. *The Mensa Think-Smart Book* will put you in the driver's seat for now and the foreseeable future. And the next time some wise guy asks you where they buried the survivors of the latest plane crash on the U.S.–Canadian border, you will recognize immediately that survivors simply don't get buried, and laugh at his ridiculous question. Ditto the one about the man hanging alone in the empty room save for the pool of water on the floor.

If you've ever had the slightest anxiety about math, *The Mensa Think-Smart Book* will ease it. It will also help you improve your ability to succeed at math problems and puzzles.

But do puzzles and games of logic, math, and language develop your intelligence? Yes, in that they are exercises for the mind. They help you increase your mental power and drive, which is as appealing as when you go on a program of physical improvement: It promises a kind of rejuvenation—a way of living better and more fully than ever before.

Finally, the authors have generously sprinkled throughout *The Mensa Think-Smart Book* little-known facts about intelligence—such as that Nicholas Murray Butler, onetime president of Columbia University, was the last person said to have known everything—and anecdotes, as well as invaluable tips on how to compute the odds at craps and blackjack so as to turn them in your favor. And last but not least, aware that even Mensans are often children at heart, we have concealed within the covers of this book a little surprise for you (see final chapter).

One final word, just in case you were wondering, which of us must answer to what—Lewis has written this introduction for the book as well as for the various chapters, coined the neologisms, and prepared the section on collecting words, and a few other little things here and there, Abbie has done all the rest. Nor could we have put everything together without the help of the members of Mensa, and the support of the American Mensa Committee. Let us also acknowledge, here and now, our debt to the late Marvin Grosswirth, who originally conceived this book.

2

WHAT IS MENSA ANYWAY?

Good question. Just follow us upstairs to the second floor at the Williams Club in New York City. A debate is taking place. An attractive dark-haired woman of not more than twenty-five is locked in combat with a seventy-year-old man who is giving no quarter. Now and then, the observers hovering over them, the way spectators hover over hard-fought chess matches, break out in applause at a point well made, or exhort their favorite with cries of "Bravo! Bravo!" Soon, the young woman, who is a mathematician, and the older man, who is a retired postal inspector, disengage from the argument at hand—"Is there a synthetic a priori?"—to move into an adjoining room, where a lecture on "Cruciverbalism" is about to begin. Simultaneously, ten or fifteen other small cliques abandon their discussions of different though equally esoteric subjects and, drinks in hand, join the two debaters in the lecture room. The people, who in appearance describe the variety of people everywhere, are Mensans. The meeting is a Mensa meeting.

The mere mention of Mensa is usually enough to elicit one of two responses—either a hackles-raised "So they have high IQs; so what?" or a cautious curiosity about standards and membership requirements. Mensa remains today as selective an organization as it has ever been.

Early in 1945, Professor Cyril Burt suggested, in a broadcast over the BBC, a panel composed of highly intelligent people. Two young Oxonians about to leave for the big city had already started a club for intelligent people, and they got in touch with Burt. Mensa has since grown into an international society of approximately seventy thousand members in some thirty-five countries. Each year, in fact, about thirty thousand people attempt to qualify for membership, which has but one qualification—an intelligence test score higher than that of 98 percent of the general population.

Yet Mensa is egalitarian, proscribing no applicants on the basis of race, creed, color, or religious conviction. Its constitution avers that its purposes are to conduct research in psychology and social science, to identify and foster human intelligence for the benefit of humanity, and to provide opportunities for social contacts among its members.

But by the very criterion that Mensa uses to cull its membership from the masses, it has identified itself, unfortunately, with the ugly morass of myth and contumely that, of late, enshrouds the subject of IQ. Further befouling the surrounding atmosphere is the fact that Sir Cyril Burt, who served as honorary president of Mensa, was a leading exponent of the thesis that intelligence is primarily a function of genetic inheritance, and is little influenced by environment. Burt was accused of everything from deliberately falsifying his research to fostering the cause of elitism, and these angry fulminations, in some eyes, blemished the name of Mensa, although these were his personal views and not those of the organization.

Still, there are busy, intelligent, and involved people who have no nagging doubts that they are able to qualify for membership but resist enlisting their intelligence for display as they would resist pinning their bank account to their lapel. To them, Mensa exists for the pedants and peacocks of the intellectual community, the mental exhibitionists who fatuously boast of their ability in an era of accomplishment. In the dissenters' view, intelligence is a tool to be used in life, not a badge worn with pride as an end in itself.

Are these criticisms valid? Yes and no. While some members undoubtedly bask in the afterglow of their intellectual endowment, most do not. Former Mensa chairman Marvin Grosswirth admitted that "many people join Mensa to see if they can make it, but once in, they stay on for other reasons." Mensa provides a social and intellectual outlet for its members, a change from the sameness and sometime sterility of their everyday lives. Many of these members do not have a string of academic credentials that entitle them to attend various high-powered colloquia and lectures. On the job, at home, and about town, they keep their brains in check. At Mensa gatherings, they are able to stretch themselves intellectually in an atmosphere of warm camaraderie and mutual respect.

But Mensa is not just an intellectual "freescape," a collection of madcaps and wags. It supports important work in the social sciences through the Mensa Education and Research Foundation (MERF), which carries out educational and research projects, not the least of whose projects is the ongoing search for a better definition of what intelligence may be. Also to Mensa's credit, many of its members happily concur with the view of Stephen J. Gould that intelligence is not an entity subject to quantification, but rather an unprogrammed and wondrously complex set of different human capabilities, or with Howard Gardner's notion of multiple intelligences. IQ to these members is nothing more than an admission ticket to a society that they enjoy. MERF also manages the Mensa Scholarship Program for postsecondary education students. Grants are awarded on the basis of motivation and goal direction with no regard for other considerations, not even Mensa membership. In addition, MERF also publishes the *Mensa Research Journal,* to which anyone may subscribe. Since Mensa is entirely composed of ex-gifted children it comprises a built-in test group for research in that field. Awards are also given to published research in the field of giftedness.

Perhaps the most visible and successful function of Mensa is the operation of its Special Interest Groups, called SIGs for short. There are literally hundreds of different SIGs, reflecting the myriad interests and needs of the Mensans, be they Esperanto, motorcycling, or Postal Diplomacy (a game). Members planning to travel have but to write SIGHT, the group responsible for hospitality, in advance, and arrangements are made to ensure an enjoyable stay, and, if desired, the company of fellow Mensans.

Just who are the Mensans? They are Isaac Asimov, science writer, and Sergei, sewer inspector; the late Buckminster Fuller, global engineer, and Patty Jacobson, truckdriver; entertainer Theodore Bikel and Middle Eastern dancer and professor Morocco (née Caroline Dinicu, whose reported IQ compares favorably with Albert Einstein's, and with most bowling scores); James Fairbanks, an Olympic competitor; Susan Clough, Ex-President Carter's secretary; and Donald Petersen, the chairman of the Ford Motor Company. In short, Mensans may be the butcher, the baker or the candlestick maker; lawyers and criminals (several convicted murderers are Mensans)—the endless migration of intelligent people from every backwater of humanity, who, for reasons as diverse as themselves, share a desire to find one another.

Most Mensans agree that IQ tests are fallible instruments, measuring a concept that has yet to be adequately defined. And they bristle at the suggestion that membership in Mensa is tantamount to being certified as a genius, as if it were somehow ennobling or would assure them a discount at the supermarket.

In the final analysis, Mensa remains a colorful and controversial society, dedicated to the proposition that intelligent people have a need to associate with other intelligent people.

Now that you know just what Mensa is, read on and learn how to think smart, as a Mensan would.

3

WORDS, WORDS,
AND MORE WORDS

Mensans love words. If nothing else, most Mensans consider themselves wordsmiths. They have read Aristotle and Korzybski and Wittgenstein ad nauseam, and are as familiar with Occam's razor as most people are with a Schick or a Remington. Mention that a game of Dictionary is being played at your home of an evening, and Mensans will come out of the woodwork the way roaches do for leftover crumbs.

Communication is also important to Mensans. They are aware that miscommunication between a student and a teacher could spell failure; between a husband and a wife, divorce; between the United States and the U.S.S.R., the end of mankind. So they are especially careful about using words.

Psychologists have established a positive correlation between a large vocabulary and both high intelligence and success in life. Mensans know this and want to succeed as much as anyone else. As a consequence they are constantly striving to expand their store of verbal knowledge.

In their spare time, Mensans love nothing better than to play with anagrams and palindromes, clerihews, oxymorons and univocalics. Most know the difference between entropy and lacunae, between a funambulist and an enchiridion. A few of them even use terms like "cyranosia," love of long noses, and "vidigital," the sign of victory made by holding two fingers in a "V," popularized by Winston Churchill and Richard Nixon. Don't even pretend that you know those last two words—you couldn't. They were created by a Mensan "lexicraftologist," who makes a living designing new words for the carriage trade. His clients say his words have a certain ring to them, a certain *je ne sais quoi,* easily spotted by cognoscenti and collectors, which is why they are willing to pay through the nose for them. But as privileged readers of *The Mensa Think-Smart Book,* you are entitled to a preview of many new words from his 1986 list, and even some clues to creating your own. Perhaps one day a word that you learned how to coin here will find its way into the language and earn you a kind of immortality!

In the pages to come, we will show you ways to increase your vocabulary geometrically as if it were a growth investment—which, incidentally, it is—as well as how to fabricate new words, or neologisms, to use and play with. Difficult anagrams and palindromes, maybe even rebuses, will become putty in your hands. Think how much money you can make during coffee break with word games at the office! In any event, we believe you will be wiser if not wealthier for what you learn, and have no doubt but that you will enjoy what we have in store. Read on, and learn to think smart with words.

VOCABULARY

Your vocabulary is the single best mark of your intelligence. This may sound like overstatement, but large numbers of research studies show that vocabulary correlates more highly with intelligence than does any other individual factor measured on IQ tests. In short, if you want to think better, increase your vocabulary.

How can you add to your arsenal of words? One way is to learn prefixes, suffixes and root forms galore—a method followed in some college classes and self-help books— so you can "decode" words you don't know.

We have not followed this approach for several reasons. For one thing, most people simply won't sit down and memorize even five words out of context each day. In addition, words learned in this manner are soon forgotten. If you don't see or use them in sentences, they don't "belong" to you. Do you remember committing lists of foreign words to memory, and then promptly forgetting them because you failed to use the language every day? Even people raised bilingually may later have trouble recalling a tongue if they have no occasion to speak it as adults. Like a muscle, language atrophies unless flexed with constant use.

One Norwegian-born friend of ours came to this country at age three to live with relatives who spoke only English, and never spoke Norwegian again until she returned at the age of 35 to visit. "After a few days," she said, "the words came flooding back, and I was able to dredge up words and sentences from memory. But I couldn't understand why everybody I spoke to laughed at me. Eventually, my elderly grandmother told me very gently that I was talking Norwegian baby talk and saying the equivalent of 'Me wanna drink of wawa.'"

Naturally. She had not used the language since she was three, and that's the way she spoke back then. Lacking constant and daily vocal exercise, she had not improved. The same is true of English vocabulary. Without repeated effort, you won't gain any ground. But practicing every day sounds dreary and intimidating. As any college professor can tell you, even motivated graduate students have trouble with drill and repetition on a daily basis.

If you choose to memorize lists of prefixes and suffixes, or even entire words, there are plenty of books to help you. We offer here a more practical and entertaining plan of action for boosting your verbal know-how:

Step 1. Select a daily newspaper or magazine that you do not ordinarily read. If you normally favor a science magazine, try one that specializes in literary criticism. If you don't read book or art reviews, or keep up with financial news, start doing so.

Step 2. On a list such as the one below, copy each word you run across that is new to you. (That's the purpose of reading in an unfamiliar area, of course.) Next, guess the word's meaning and jot it down, basing it on context and whatever acquaintance you have with similar words. Then, when you get a chance, copy the dictionary definition, as briefly as you can.

Step 3. Review your new word "finds" at least once a week. If you read a given publication for any length of time, you'll soon discover that the same words tend to recur. Consult your list regularly, and see if you recognize or have mastered any words you came across the first time.

Step 4. When you have checked off every once-unfamiliar word on your list that you know now, you're ready to move on. Try another section of the same magazine or a new periodical. If you've been reading film criticism, pick up music or home furnishings. Once you have learned all the new words in that magazine, section or newspaper, go on to another. (This routine has an added benefit. By exposing you to previously uncharted areas, it's bound to enlarge your "information quotient" and expertise, along with your vocabulary.)

Step 5. Review your entire list regularly. Remember, unless you use the words, see them often, or review them at frequent intervals, you are apt to forget them.

Here is the first part of Step 1. Fill in the blanks and get to work on this key "think-smart" technique:

READING DIARY

My regular newspaper _____

My newly chosen newspaper _____

My current favorite magazine _____

My new selection _____

New section of newspaper to read _____

Date started new reading materials _____

Second week _____

If mastered, new selection _____

Third week, date started _____

If mastered, new selection _____

Fourth week, date started _____

If mastered, new selection _____

New Words List for Week 1

Word _____ My original idea _____

Dictionary definition _____

Word _____ My original idea _____

Dictionary definition _____

Word _____ My original idea _____

Dictionary definition _____

Word _____ My original idea _____

Dictionary definition _____

Word _____ My original idea _____

Dictionary definition _____

Now that you have learned the basics, here are some techniques for review. A chart is given below, on which you can record your progress. At the beginning of each week, you may be able to check off a. and b., for example. Checking off these two items would show familiarity with the word, but still not mastery of it. When you know all of the uses of the word listed in item c., and can check that letter off also, you will know that you have really conquered the new word. You should make up a chart such as the sample given here for each week. At the end of the week, if the word is now in your vocabulary, you have finished with that word. You can then start on another. If you still have not mastered the word, make up the same chart for Week 2, and continue this way until you have learned your new word thoroughly.

Week 1

	Word 1	Word 2	Word 3	Word 4	Word 5
	ovoid	vulpine	glabrous	hispid	epicene
a. I recognize this word when I see it in an unfamiliar context, but I still have to look up the meaning.	×	×	×	×	×
b. I remember the exact meaning when I see it.	×	×	×	×	×
c. I can recall the word, can use it comfortably in speech or writing, and can think of it as a synonym when I come across a word that means much the same.	×	×	×	×	×

This chart shows one week's work on the five words indicated where all five have been mastered. Now you should make your own chart for words you want to learn. If you practice this technique faithfully (on more than five words a week, if you wish), you will find your vocabulary increasing steadily.

Other pointers: Get a special dictionary of synonyms and antonyms, and look these up for every unknown word you find. (Knowing the opposites of words helps reinforce their meaning for you and can stretch your vocabulary even further.) When you're reading technical items, it may sometimes be necessary to look up the word in *parts*. For example, with "pyrophosphate," you might have to refer to "pyro-" and then "phosphate." Or you may have to check the definitions of several related words before you get a sense of the meaning of your primary word. *Don't quit.*

Verbal Trickery

There are also gamelike ways to enhance your vocabulary. For example, suppose you were given a challenge like this: Take the ten letters EVESIISRPM and make two common English words using all ten of them. How would you go about it?

The first thing you might think about is word endings and beginnings. The jumble contains three letters—IVE—that often end words, so start with that. Make up a line of ten dashes and put IVE on the last three. Now look at the remaining letters. Do they suggest anything to you? If you are word wise, you will see that the letters could make a double S before the IVE. Try it. Now you have SSIVE. At this point you may get an "aha" reaction and "see" a word. Perhaps it is IMPRESSIVE. Yes, it fits! How about the other word? Start working with the letters and look for some compatible pairs or groupings. You have ER there, and IM and a P. ER is a fairly common combination. What do you know that starts with a P and has ER? Try PER and see what happens. Again, there should be an "aha" as you see the word PERMISSIVE. This is how to work out long word puzzles when you are given mixed-up letters.

Now try these two. (Answers are at the end of the chapter):

1. Make two common eight-letter words from
   IISSNTDE.   — — — — — — — —

                                                — — — — — — — —

2. Make three common eight-letter English
   words from DSREGINI.   — — — — — — — —

                                                — — — — — — — —

                                                — — — — — — — —

How about crossword puzzles? These are a bit more difficult because the words have to be checked in two directions and all you are given at first are definitions. Suppose you have to find an eight-letter word meaning "chanced" and all you know is that it starts with H. You know the word is going to end with ED, because its definition is in the past tense. (At any event, it is most likely to end that way). So all you need is a clue to a six-letter word, starting with H, that means chance. What's a synonym for "chance"? "Gamble"? No, that doesn't start with H. Perhaps "hazard." We now have a six-letter word beginning with H. Try it, and see if you can match any of the intersecting words—especially one that crosses the Z in the middle. If you can match up cross-words, either down or across, you have solved that particular word.

There is another more complex type of puzzle, also a crossword, that uses puns and anagrams. The London *Times* publishes these as a regular feature (they are known simply as London *Times* Crossword Puzzles) and aficionados are legion. Cleverness (or sheer perversity!) is the keynote here, as one example will show. Suppose you found the "definition": "An edible French car, you have." The answer is ESCARGOT. These may not be everybody's cup of tea!

Then there is the Double-Crostic, in which, when you fill in all the words, you have a quotation.

Another fiendish game is the palindrome—a word, sentence, paragraph, or poem that reads identically backward and forward, or forward and backward, depending on your mood. The first known English palindrome is attributed to John Taylor, a seventeenth-century poet. "Lewd did I live, evil I did dwel." Of course, according to modern spelling practice, this is not a palindrome, but if Shakespeare could spell his own name three different ways on one document, we can accept this as a palindrome of the same era.

Palindromes were not invented in the seventeenth century. John Taylor may have known the lawyer's motto—in Latin, "Si nummi immunis," which means, approximately, "If you pay me, I'll get you free." Many other languages have palindromes also. A Dutch palindrome is "Neder sit wort; trow tis reden," which translates into "The word is inferior, the intellect endures."

With these examples before you, you will realize that the trick to composing palindromes is to find words, or parts of words, that can be read forward or backward. In English, such words as "reviled" and "deliver" are often used. You may also find use for those famous palindrome characters Otto and Anna. As can be seen from the Latin example above, and the one that follows, you can use parts of words also, as in "Sit on a potato pan, Otis."

Try to compose your own palindrome from the following clues. This palindrome is the motto of a gambler who bets only on red or black at the roulette wheel. What would that gambler say?

Still another vocabulary-building word game, apparently invented by Lewis Carroll, is called Ladders, or Word Ladders. In this game, you could be asked to go, for example, from SLOW to FAST by changing one letter at a time, each change producing a good English word. One possibility is SLOW,

SLOT, SOOT, COOT, COST, CAST, FAST. The more words you know, the more variants on each ladder you can find. For some word ladders, an extensive vocabulary is required.

3.   Now try one for yourself. This one should be reasonably easy, as it takes only 5 changes: Go from PLAY to ROOM in 6 changes. There are several ways to do this. At least one way involves some rather unusual words.

P L A Y

– – – –

– – – –

– – – –

– – – –

– – – –

R O O M

The answer is at the end of the chapter.

Here are some additional questions for practice. Answers follow at the end of the chapter.

4.   Give two eight-letter words—one beginning with S, the other with T—that could mean "shone brightly" or "glittered."

– – – – – – – –

– – – – – – – –

5.   Give three synonyms for "fast," one beginning with S, one with C, and one with T.

6.   Can you go from GLOW to WORM in six steps? and from BIRD to NEST in five?

G L O W   B I R D

– –   – – – –

– – – –   – – – –

– – – –   – – – –

– – – –   – – – –

– – – – –   N E S T

W O R M

Collecting Words

One of the ways many Mensans learn new words and build their vocabularies is by collecting words. Usually the words are rare or exotic, though sometimes they are just words the collector doesn't know. If they are also useful, they serve a double purpose, just as any useful collectible would. Words are also inexpensive to collect, easy to maintain, and fun to display.

In order to motivate you into starting a collection, we have prevailed on a prominent Mensan to lend us his collection to include in the book. It is small in quantity, but rich in texture and diversity. The likelihood is that you won't know more than 20 percent of these words—most Mensans wouldn't—but if you do, all the more power to you. Naturally, we are not giving you the definitions, since half the fun in a collection such as this is digging up the meaning. In this way the meanings will stay with you longer. Most learning experiences do when you have had to work at them.

After you have started your own collection we invite you to send us a copy of your words care of the publisher, so we can take some pleasure in having started you on your way. Here now are the words:

ululations	rutilant	anlage
favonian	regorche	stele
sudorific	louch	pudency
carious	hirple	susurrant
quare	circinate	subaqueous
incondite	abiogenesis	transhuman
callipygian	cadge	palanquin
preprandial	funambulist	lee
tumid	farouche	onomastics
condign	pelf	tramontane
paraclete	paludal	glissading
adscititious	hagridden	sinople
elucubrate	hajj	cachectic
enchiridion	objurgate	gallimaufry

feeze	mullion	globose
demotic	parlous	tessera
nonce	tsunami	gloriole
keratinous	lacunae	orts
enchorial	portcullis	falciform
screed	sough	leporine
epigone	crenellated	soubrette
plantigrade	diluvial	glaucous
trull	deracinate	raddle
calcimine	freshet	epicene
cicatrix	eponymous	exordium
bolus	prognathous	prodromal
chiffonier	bullyrag	gules
animadvert	immanent	gride
purblind	parturition	tarn
wen	avatar	equivoque
sere	hysteroid	cozenage
maundering	anneal	dysphoria
uxorial	skookum	macerate
dorty	torminous	vespertine
profluent	clyster	toponym
rictus	claviform	vermifuge
ylem	conation	supertenuous
osculate	umiak	
otiose	coot	
ossIfy	mala fide	
farrago	palter	
swale	gobemouche	
poniard	misoneist	
caravansary	diseur	
minatory	suigenderism	

Betwixtors

As promised, we have prevailed upon our resident lexicraftologist to reveal his 1986 list of new words. They are previewed here expressly for *The Mensa Think-Smart Book,* and cannot yet be seen anywhere else. Thus they are betwixtors, betwixt and between being newly minted and common coinage. Should you encounter one of these neologisms in a conversation, in a newspaper, or even on the side of a subway car, please report it immediately to Mensa headquarters.

In the meantime, try to craft some words of your own that match our expert's, both in quality and in imagination. Then use your own new words in place of "you know" and "uhhh" in everyday situations. You will not only appear smarter, you will be smarter. Here's how:

Either begin with a word of your own invention that you know has no known meaning (look it up in the unabridged dictionary to be sure), such as "whiptide," and give it meaning. For example, whiptide = late afternoon ocean waves whipped to a frenzy by the wind. Or find something that should have a single word to express it, but doesn't, and create one. "Cornipsis," for example, was coined by our expert to describe the act of pinching a child's cheek. This sadistic act, usually engaged in by well-meaning aunts and uncles, hitherto had no word to call its own. Now it does. "My aunt performed cornipsis on me when I was ten. It still smarts." Study the following; then create your own.

ARAMANTH   The fragrance of charcoal
BARBATRON   An electronic barbecue grill of the future
BERGLYNT   The practiced smile that accompanies the greeting "Hi, how're you?"
BETWIXTOR   Something betwixt and between
BIANDROVOROUS   Eating one's meat rare or well-done
CAPULOUS   Critically aware
CLIMACTERODE   The state of being on the way down
CORNIPSIS   The pinching of a child's cheek, usually engaged in by well-meaning aunts and uncles
CYRANOSIA   Love of long noses
DOLORIL   A countertranquilizer used to produce melancholy in manics
DUCQUINESQUE   Ducklike

EARWITNESS One who listens to something that is going on

E-PLAN That plan which follows D-plan but precedes F-plan

EPONIUM State of attracting name-calling

EXORN To decorate from the outside

FATANGELO Epithet used by Angelo's wife

FENSTERPHOBIA Fear of being attacked by a man named Fenster

FESILE Seriously felicitous

FLAMANOUS Provocative, inflammatory

GOLSE To push into line

GRUNCH To rend or tear by force

HORPITH Name given to the sound *uhh*, usually uttered while one searches for a thought or word

JANORIL A miniature sunflower seldom found in either hemisphere. It was discovered in 1877 by the German botanist Gottfried von Duberstung. In 1908, the drug misaril was synthesized from the stamen of the janoril flower and was used to treat rampant pinheadism. Due to the rarity of the janoril plant, production of misaril was terminated in 1909, which explains the continued virulence of R.P.

JILK The residue left on one's body by suntan oil

KISANTEL Coquette

KNOCKWOOD The wood of the superstition tree

LACTOPOID Milk drinker

LAMPOID Resembling the shape of a lamp

MALLOMARIC Of or pertaining to Mallomars

MEDULLAPHOBIA Irrational fear of the medulla oblongata

MOLOQUIAL Conversationally obsessive

MORBURGE State of being tuned out

NE DÉJÀ VU PAS *Fr.* Feeling that you have not been someplace before

OBTOIL Unsuccessful labor

OLVIDESE The feeling of having forgotten something

OMNIS PRO DORFUNKEN *L.* All for dorfunken

ONIONATE Multilayered

PALINOSIS *Path.* A marked tendency to develop hangnails

PROMATIONAL Of, or pertaining to, a promise

TERSIFY To make shorter or more succinct

VOLULATE To talk incessantly, chatter

7. Can you come up with meanings for the following neologisms? We've assigned definitions that seem apposite to us, but don't look until you've allowed your own imagination free reign.

MAUVINE ⎯⎯⎯⎯⎯⎯⎯⎯⎯⎯⎯⎯⎯

PICOIOI ⎯⎯⎯⎯⎯⎯⎯⎯⎯⎯⎯⎯⎯

LASSITOSIS ⎯⎯⎯⎯⎯⎯⎯⎯⎯⎯⎯

MALVECT ⎯⎯⎯⎯⎯⎯⎯⎯⎯⎯⎯⎯

ABTENSILE ⎯⎯⎯⎯⎯⎯⎯⎯⎯⎯⎯

SCUR ⎯⎯⎯⎯⎯⎯⎯⎯⎯⎯⎯⎯⎯⎯

BLOMBEY ⎯⎯⎯⎯⎯⎯⎯⎯⎯⎯⎯⎯

VERTIFORM ⎯⎯⎯⎯⎯⎯⎯⎯⎯⎯⎯

PUNCTOMINIOUS ⎯⎯⎯⎯⎯⎯⎯⎯⎯

PALINDROMANIA ⎯⎯⎯⎯⎯⎯⎯⎯⎯

PENULTIMATUM ⎯⎯⎯⎯⎯⎯⎯⎯⎯

NULLUM SERIOSIS ⎯⎯⎯⎯⎯⎯⎯⎯

ANSWERS

1. IISSNTDE: INSISTED;   TIDINESS

2. DSREGINI: DESIRING;   RESIDING;   RINGSIDE

3. PLAY, PLAT, BLAT, BOAT, BOOT, BOOM, ROOM

4. SPARKLED;   TWINKLED

5. SECURED;   CONSTANT;   TIGHT

6. GLOW, SLOW, SLOT, SOOT, SORT, WORT, WORM

   BIRD, BIND, BEND, BENT, BEST, NEST

Of course, there may be other ways, possibly even shorter. These word ladders are excellent ways to improve your acquaintance with odd, shorter words. If you want to try a harder one, for which we are NOT giving a solution, although one exists, try going from BUTTER to CHEESE.

MAUVINE Purplish

PICOIOI   The sound made by coiled springs

LASSITOSIS   Chronic laziness or boredom

MALVECT   Cast aspersions

ABTENSILE   Tending to lose one's grip

SCUR   To mark up or blemish

BLOMBEY   Fluff- or down-lined hood

VERTIFORM   Upright

PUNCTOMINIOUS   Precise to the point of pettiness

PALINDROMANIA   Fanatic love of puzzles (esp. word puzzles)

PENULTIMATUM   Almost an ultimatum

NULLUM SERIOSIS   *L.* Nothing serious

Of course, we have not forgotten to give you the gambler's palindrome: NEVER ODD OR EVEN.

If you figured out that one, just for fun, you might try to think about what the famous chef said when he was asked to prepare the appetizer of prosciutto, melon, and a lemon slice. Of course: NO MELONS NO LEMON.

These are a good way to provide innocent amusement as well as fiendish torture. Palindrome composing provides good thinking—or should we say, DAFT FAD!

4

DEMYSTIFYING MATH

Quick, what did John Von Neumann, Stanislaw Ulam, David Hilbert, Jules-Henri Poincaré, and Norbert Wiener all have in common?

You guessed it: each of them knew how to think smart mathematically without having read this book. Just how this was possible we are not certain, but we suspect it had something to do with genetics and the fact that none of them suffered from math anxiety.

In this chapter we will show you how to overcome your math anxiety if you have it. No more "Yikes, it's the square root of five! Get it away from me quick. Help! Help!" No more cold sweats as you contemplate having to multiply or divide something larger than a pizza, especially in your head. In "Demystifying Math" we will show you how to approach mathematics in such a way that it becomes fun and appealing rather than cold and forbidding. We will also teach you many practical applications of math that will help you in your everyday life.

Do you play cards? Poker, or bridge? Wouldn't you like to know your chances of drawing all thirteen spades—or any other suit—in one hand? For the record, the odds are one in 158,753,389,899. So if you've heard any stories about a game in which all four players had thirteen cards in a single suit . . . Need I say more?

How about the chances of getting a royal flush in a poker game? Here your odds are somewhat better, one in 649,739—nothing to hang your hat on, but better than trying to assemble thirteen cards of one suit. Maybe you'd be better off with dice—say, shooting craps. The probability of consistent winning rolls in craps by seven, eleven, or point is actually six in twenty-five for one win, down to one in 582 for nine.

Of course these are just some interesting odds statistics that may help you in a casino. If you want to learn to figure others for yourself, however—the odds on the state lottery, for example, or those on your local bingo game, or even the odds on the toss of a coin—read on in this chapter.

People spend millions of dollars foolishly every day of the year because they are ignorant of odds and how to figure and use them. Don't you be one of these losing statistics.

In "Demystifying Math" we will also teach you new ways to calculate numbers quickly in your head. Of course, if you are the type that carries a computer around with you at all times, the way some individuals carry huge stereo "boxes," you can skip calculation and go right to the section on mind reading and parlor math. You'll be the hit of the party—or at least one in three of you will be. Ready now—one, two, one, two, one . . .

MAGIC STUNTS

Research shows that people fear mathematics more than any other subject. Although it is hardly acceptable to be "dumb" in other areas, many individuals actually pride themselves on their inability to do numbers. Think of all the jokes about balancing checkbooks. And while it is true that statistically girls tend to score lower on math tests above the elementary level than boys, it is also true that for a long time women were not encouraged in the field of math. An interesting exception to this rule is Byron's daughter, who developed the original calculator (see Chapter 9, "High-IQ Trivia").

We also tend to fear what we don't know. If you understand that numbers are symbols, just as words are, they will no longer seem so intimidating. And if you also learn to play with numbers, get comfortable with them, do tricks and games, so that you see how easy it is to manipulate them, the little anxiety you have left will be dissipated.

Because so many people are intimidated by math and have blown its difficulties out of proportion in their minds, they tend to regard as "smart" anyone who can do numbers fast and easily. You can learn to do some of these calculations, as well as tricks and games, fast and easily through aids and shortcuts we will teach you. And your reward for mastering the chapter, with its exercises and games, will be surprise and admiration from your friends and acquaintances. This will tend to reduce still further whatever residual anxiety you had about mathematics.

There is absolutely nothing that does more for your self-esteem than having other people think you are smart. And there is nothing that makes people think you are smart more than an ability to play with numbers in ways that your audience does not know.

Tricks and games may not be of any practical significance in terms of teaching you math. They *are* of enormous importance in raising your self-esteem. If you can manipulate numbers to the bewilderment of your audience—most of whom can't do so—you will acquire a reputation as a sharp thinker. This in turn will convince you, if you need convincing, that you are indeed a smart person, especially in the math line. As we've said, math anxiety is so common as to be almost universal (except among mathematicians, naturally).

Tossing off a few of the tricks and games that follow will help gain you a reputation. In so doing, you will boost your own self-esteem, and that's a large part of ability.

One mathematical stunt has been used as the basis for many trick questions and puzzles, but the process is absurdly simple. Ask your subject (but try it out first yourself) for any number less than 1000, whose first and last numbers are different. Take, for example, 789. Once you have the number, transpose it. In this case, you have 987. Take the difference between the two numbers, reverse the difference, and add it to the original difference. You will always get 1089. Of course, if you get a two-digit difference, don't forget the zero.

Example:
$$695$$
$$-596$$
$$099 \ (+990)$$

Here's a sample of this peculiar bit of number magic.

789, transposed is 987.
$$987$$
$$- \ 789$$
$$198$$

Following the procedure outlined, you now take 198, transpose it, and add the resultant number to the original difference:

$$198$$
transposed: $$891$$
$$1089$$ As promised, the answer is 1089.

Try it yourself on any three-digit number whose first and last numbers differ. Work it out now for the following numbers: 645; 327; 789; 546. (And don't forget to use the zero when necessary.)

You can always make this procedure more enticing by building a story around it, or converting it to money (always a fascinating subject), more than a dollar and less than ten. It's still the same.

If you choose to do this as a magic or mind-reading trick, a word of warning. Give the directions to your subject just as we have given them to you here. (We assume you will have memorized the five steps carefully.) When you have finished your instructions, have your subject add a predetermined number. For example, you might say at the end, "and then add eleven." This, of course, would give you 1100. Or you could say, "and then add fifty." The purpose of this final and totally unnecessary step is to give you credibility. If you are doing this trick at a party, and are asked to repeat it, you don't want all the answers to come out 1089, do you? It is highly unlikely that any will think to subtract from each answer the last number you gave, and realize that 1089 is the constant. It is, however, possible that somebody else will also know this trick. Against that there is no defense.

Factors of 9 produce odd results also. Look at the following pyramid:

$$0 \times 9 + 1 = 1$$

$$1 \times 9 + 2 = 11$$

$$12 \times 9 + 3 = 111$$

$$123 \times 9 + 4 = 1111$$

$$1234 \times 9 + 5 = 11111$$

This pattern can be followed all the way through to the final number, which is:

$$123456789 \times 9 + 10 = 1111111111$$

You can make up a trick story or game with this set of tables, too, knowing in advance what your answer will be.

Of course, there is always the old "birthday trick" to amuse and mystify friends and party guests. This is simplicity itself, provided you can add and subtract (and multiply). Let's try it for July 3.

Tell the subject—or victim—to take the month of his or her birth, starting with January as 1. Then add the next higher number. For example, if the subject's birthday is July, that would be month number 7. The subject would then add the number 8 to that, getting a sum of 15 (8 is the next higher number).

You then tell your subject to multiply the result by 5. That gives a total of 75. Then tell him to multiply by 10, and add the date of birth. That will give an answer of 750, plus 3, or 753. You then mentally subtract 50, and there you are—7 03.

Here are some examples worked out for you:

Oct. 10: 10 + 11 = 21; multiplied by 5, 105; multiplied by 10, 1050; add the date of 10; then mentally subtract 50; and you have 10 10.

Dec. 21: 12 + 13 = 25. Multiplied by 5, this is 125. Multiplied by 10, it is then 1250; with the date added, it is 1271. You mentally subtract 50, and there is 12 21.

It is quite simple, but usually produces a sensation. We can't guarantee that it will astonish your friends—it worked every time we tried it in terms of surprising the subject.

There are many variations on this. We developed this particular formula, as far as we can determine. It is quick, easy, and requires minimal concentration on the part of the doer.

Not surprisingly, since we planned it that way, this brings us to probability. This is the study of the chances that a particular event will occur. We use probability every day, in dozens of ways, even if we don't realize that we are doing it. Buying stocks instead of bonds, making business decisions, buying insurance, and myriads of other activities all involve the probability that an event will or will not occur. We are so accustomed to thinking about this almost automatically that many of us don't realize there is a technical basis for it. Gamblers, of course, use probability all the time for betting. Certain stock-market forecasters use probability charts for their predictions. When you buy or don't buy a warranty on your TV set or other appliance, you are using the rules of probability. What are the chances that your appliance will break down before the original guarantee expires? We usually base our decisions on our own experience. Big companies don't, they base their prices for warranties on extensive statistical studies. Probability affects all of us, every day, and you really should have a basic idea of it just to be able to estimate if you are getting a fair deal.

Birthdays provide an amusing real-life example of probability. For instance, if you have twenty-five people in a room, what is the approximate probability that any two will have the same birth date (not year, just month and day). Would you bet that any two will have the same birthday? The formula, which applies for many events, is as follows: With any two people in the room, there are 364 chances out of 365 that they will not have the same birthday. A third person reduces the chances to 363/365 that the dates won't match, and so on down the line. When you have finished with your list, you multiply all the probabilities together. If you have twenty-five people in the room, the chances are very much better than even that two will have the same birth date. You would make money if you bet even money that any two would have the same birthday; perhaps not each time, but over the long run.

If you take the entire row of probabilities, the formula will look like this, carried out:

$$\frac{364 \times 363 \times 362 \times 361 \times 360}{365 \times 365 \times 365 \times 365 \times 365}.$$

and so on, which, when multiplied out, and subtracted from P = 1, will give you somewhat over 50%. You don't have to know the formula, you just have to know a few odds. With 25 people, the odds are considerably better than 50%. With 40 people, the probably is about 89% that two or more have the same birthday.

Now how about the tossed coin? What are the odds of its turning up heads and what are the odds of its turning up tails? Suppose you place a substantial bet on heads twice in a row? What is the probability of getting heads twice in a row? That's simple, if you know. It's one out of two, each time, no matter how often you toss. So the formula is $\frac{1}{2} \times \frac{1}{2}$ or $\frac{1}{4}$. You have only one chance in four of having that sequence—don't bet on it!

In other instances, the same type of mathematical probabilities comes up. Say you are making a batch of identical widgets. To help in cutting them, you line them up in clamps (or jigs). If you have a specific number of holders in a row, you need to know exactly how many widgets will fill the holders economically and with the smallest possible number of refills. Suppose you have holders with two, three, and five holes, and you want to know how many widgets you can make with the most economical use of time and energy. You simply multiply $2 \times 3 \times 5$, and you come up with 30. That tells you that you can work in multiples of thirty for maximum economy. You'll find problems like this in real life, in many do-it-yourself situations.

Guesstimating is the handiest of math skills allowing you to tell, by common sense and inspection, approximately what an amount should be; or at least the number range into which the answer will fall. If your checkbook shows three stubs, each with an amount under $20, you should know just by looking that you are not going to have a total deficit of more than $60. That's simple. But so is multiplying $63 by 15. You should know that your answer will be more than $900 but less than $1,000. What's the value of guesstimating? That's simple too. If you don't guesstimate, you could be off by one or two zeros and not notice it! One of the leading business magazines recently reported that almost all of the major mathematical errors made with computers involved a failure to recognize that the answer was off by one or more decimal places.

EXERCISES

These mathematical exercises will train, amuse, and help you. The answers follow.

1. Your friend, who is a bit of a mathematician, is willing to toss a coin to decide who will pay for dinner in a very expensive restaurant. He makes you an offer. If heads comes up two times out of three (no more and no less), he will pay. Is he being generous?

2. If six widgets and two whatsits cost $10, and six whatsits and three widgets cost $15, what do a widget and a whatsit cost? (You can solve this problem by three methods—including some application of common sense.)

3. You and your family have several cars. All but two are station wagons, all but two are sports cars, and all but two are sedans. How many cars do you have altogether?

4. Magic squares are several thousand years old. For all that time, they have provided a chance for people to test their wits. Now try this classic square. The magic square below uses nine different numbers. All of the numbers add up to 15, whether you add along the vertical or horizontal, or along the long diagonals. Hint: No number is smaller than 3, nor larger than 7.

5. Two antique dealers were gloating over their purchases when the third member of their crew came in. "We did very well at the flea market," they told their partner. "One of us found five antique TV sets, guaranteed to be over one hundred years old, and the other found seven, so when we split evenly, we'll each have four. And you can be glad they only cost us $1,200! And each for exactly the same price." How much did the third partner pay each of the other two?

6. This example uses both mathematics and logic. You walk, at three miles per hour, for twelve miles. You return, after resting, at a quick run of six miles per hour. What is your average speed?

7.   On one of those islands that exist only in puzzle books, a traveler met a stranger who was bragging about how many horses he had. The stranger with the horses was willing to make a large bet that the traveler could not tell him how many. The traveler took him up on it, and the horse-owner said, "If one fourth, one fifth, and one sixth of the total number of horses were added together, there would be a total of thirty-seven." How many horses were there to start?

8.   You're a very careful person, but just this once you didn't count your money when you cashed a check. You count your money later and, being mathematically inclined, realize that if you take away sixty-five cents, you will have exactly double the amount of your original check, because the cashier has given you dollars for cents and cents for dollars. Your original check was for less than twenty dollars, but just how much was it, anyway?

9.   Good heavens! Your motorboat is being dragged toward the falls! You can go back at sixteen miles per hour, but the current is pulling you toward the falls at 9 miles per hour. You are using 10 gallons of fuel per hour, you have 31 gallons left, and the only safe landing is 21 miles back upriver. Are you going to make it?

10.   A dress store owner ordered a shipment of evening gowns for his shop. When they arrived, the poor man found there had been a mistake. Half of the garments were coats, 20 percent were children's sizes, and 24 of the garments were both coats and in sizes for children. There were only 99 of the evening dresses he had ordered. How many had he ordered initially?

ANSWERS

1.   It's not really generous. By mathematical convention, two out of three means exactly that, not two or more out of three. There are only three combinations out of the possible eight that will give you two out of three exactly—HHT, HTH, THH. That gives you the proportion of three out of eight, which is not even odds.

2.   A widget costs $1 and a whatsit costs $2. This particular problem can be solved by algebra, or by trial and error, since the numbers are so small.

3.   Only three. This is a variant on a question that exists in almost all math puzzle books. All except two are station wagons, which means two are not station wagons; all except two are sports cars; which means two are not sports cars; and all except two are sedans, which means two are not sedans. You have three types of cars, and the only answer that will fit the formula is that there is one of each.

4.   In this problem you had to recognize that nothing was said about whole numbers. If you look at the answer given, you will see that each number is different, as required. (Of course, a mirror image is also correct, and there may be other solutions, if you used other fractions, but this solution is the one we are giving for an example.)

5½	6	3½
3	5	7
6½	4	4½

5.   The third friend paid each for what was received. There was a total of twelve sets at, obviously, $100 each. The one who gave one got $100, the one who gave three got $300.

6.   Your average speed is four miles per hour, and the answer is obtained quite simply. You do not divide the total of three miles per hour and six miles per hour, because that omits the distance, which must be considered. You realize that you went twenty-four miles in six hours, which, very simply, gives you four miles per hour. This is an excellent example for making you realize all the factors that must be taken into account. (For practice, make up some of this type yourself.)

7.   The stranger in question had sixty horses. This problem can be worked out either algebraically or arithmetically. (Sixty is the smallest number divisible by four, five, and six. The fractions add up to the required thirty-seven.)

8.   The original check was for $11.23. You received $23.11. If you subtract .65, you will have $22.46, which is double the $11.23 for which you made out your check.

9.   Yes. Not only will you make it, but you will have 1 gallon of gas left over. There are two factors here—the 7 miles an hour you are making against the current, which means it will take you 3 hours to go 21 miles—and the 10 gallons per hour. You have 1 gallon left out of 31 in 3 hours. (Please don't mention that when the gasoline gets that low, you may have a problem. This all happened in Math Puzzle Land, where the normal rules don't apply.)

10.   There should have been 250 evening gowns. Half were coats, which means there were 125 coats, or 50 percent. Twenty percent were children's sizes, which means 50, but of those, 24 were both coats and for children. Therefore, you must subtract the 24 from the total obtained, as these are overlapping categories. You therefore have 50 percent, plus 20 percent, plus $99 - 24 = 100$ percent.

5

THE PUZZLE OF MEMORY

Let's get serious for a moment. While even simple, one-cell bacteria have a rudimentary memory and computers (and some Mensans) have so-called memory banks, the gift of remembered experience in all its aspects is unique to man. And man is just beginning to understand how the memory works and how to train and improve it.

Essentially there are two kinds of human memory—the short- and the long-term. Short-term memory is best exemplified by the myriad of facts encountered in everyday life: telephone numbers, faces on a moving bus, the prices in jewelry store windows, the prattle of street vendors hawking their wares. Unless otherwise reinforced, the fact or impression is gone in moments.

Valuable as short-term memory may be, it is eclipsed by the vast and prodigious function of the brain's almost infinite storehouse—the long-term memory. Here, filed away in profusion, are the deposits of a lifetime's experience: the wind blowing the hair of a first love on the Ferris wheel circa late adolescence; the smell of marshmallows roasting over a bonfire at the last Mensa RG (regional gathering); the frustration of a first fall from a tricycle; the glory that went with belting a home run off Butch McConky at camp. All our memories are there, apparently waiting for retrieval. Doctors who have surgically implanted electrodes into subjects' brains have reported the release of floods of hitherto forgotten memories. So they are there.

While there is some controversy over whether the memory apparatus functions electrically (the dry theory) or chemically (the wet theory), there is little doubt that it can be improved. Neurophysiologists, psychologists, even nutritionists, concede this fact, and continue to explore new avenues of investigation.

Perhaps the most talked-about experiment in memory research, though, was begun in the late 1950s by James V. McConnell, who discovered that when a planarian, a freshwater flatworm, which is the simplest animal with a brain and true synapses, was chopped up and fed to another worm, the survivor apparently acquired some of the memory of the sacrificial victim. The book *How to Raise Your IQ by Eating Gifted Children*, by Lewis Frumkes, was a direct response to this stimulating discovery. Perhaps one day we will all be taking shots of French verbs or applied physics.

In any case, how many times have you remembered someone's face but not the name to go with it? How many times have you had a déjà vu experience, the distinct feeling that you have witnessed a place or scene before but cannot recall where or when? Lots of people can remember faces with far greater ease than names, and most have had feelings of déjà vu.

This is because many of us have better visual or pictorial memory than verbal memory. If, for example, you were shown a group of fifty pictures and then asked to recall which pictures out of a second showing of a hundred you had seen before, the chances are you would get them all correct. Amazing, but true. On the other hand, if you were given fifty telephone numbers and tested for recognition, your recollection would be likely to include a great many gaps. We tend to organize visual material so that it has meaning for us, a feat more difficult for verbal matter.

If we dumped all the books in the New York Public Library into the waiting room of Grand Central Terminal, it would take years to find any one title. But because books are catalogued, we can find that same title in a matter of minutes at the library. We can organize our minds in much the same manner through the use of mnemonic devices, or associative techniques, which we will explain, utilizing the pictorial memory. In fact, we can train our memories to accomplish feats we would never have thought possible. (I know this because I can do some of them. I can, for example, commit a list of twenty to forty objects to memory as it is read, so that if it is asked of me, I can recite any individual object out of order, or all of them backward or forward. You can do it too.—L.B.F.)

Here is one association technique you can use: First, create and commit to memory your own master list of objects. These may be anything you wish, so long as you feel comfortable with them. For example, your number one may be "boat." Number two, "cat." Number three, "fence," and so on up to twenty. Know them so thoroughly that when someone says "three," you will automatically respond with a visual image of a fence. If they said "seventeen," you would automatically, and without thinking, conjure up whatever key image your number seventeen was. Perhaps seventeen is "fish." A fish would spring immediately to mind. Learn them so that you can recite them backward or forward at will, in order, or out of order, odds, evens, whatever.

Now, when someone reads a list of items to you, you will associate each of the new items with the object on your master list. For instance, if the person says number two is "couch," you will conjure up *your* number two, which is "cat," and make a picture out of your key word and the new word—a cat curled up on a couch, say. When the person later asks you to recall number two, you will recall your master list number two, which is "cat," and remember your mental picture of the cat curled up on a couch. "Couch," you will say.

And you will be able to do the same with any of the twenty words you were asked to memorize, or however many key words you have previously committed to memory.

The first major step in improving your memory is to distribute your learning over a reasonably spaced period. If you have twenty hours to study, it will do you very little good to study all day the day before the examination. You will have far better results if you practice and learn for perhaps four hours a day for five days. According to one theory, this gives the facts a chance to enter into the long-term memory.

There is another important point. Memory seems to "consolidate" far better if you sleep after learning. That means you should time your study periods to precede sleep. It seems to be a violation of common sense to study at night, when you are tired, rather than in the morning when you are fresh and rested, but there is plenty of evidence that sleep consolidates the material you have learned, while if you study in the morning, your daily activities interrupt this process.

On the other hand, while this type of study will help you pass tests and learn current material, it may not be best for retaining facts and lists for a very long time. There is also some evidence that on puzzles and "difficult" material, it is better to persist with the problem, however long, until it is solved.

Also, you must decide whether to learn the whole set of materials at once or learn it a section at a time. Here, intelligence is an asset. The smarter you are, the better you seem to learn by studying all the material instead of part of it. If time doesn't allow this, you are better off reviewing the last section you have studied, and working in parts. That method combines the advantages of part study with whole study. You start *before* the point where you stopped learning, relearn some of the material you have already studied, and then go on to the new matter.

Of course, it would be very easy, at this point, to give you ways to spend hours memorizing lists of association words and similar stunts. After studying hard, you, too, could learn to amaze your friends by memorizing lists of twenty words (although eight are far easier, and you can always combine the lists). But that won't teach you the principles behind memorization. We're going to give you the association tricks; but more important, we'll also give you the tools you need to *want* to learn, and the principles of rewarding yourself so that memorization and learning become fun.

While there are many books available on memory improvement, we especially recommend Harry Lorayne's *The Memory Book* and Bruno Furst's *Stop Forgetting*. You can just as easily invent your own mnemonic devices and associations as you go along; you are limited only by your imagination and your willingness to try. Now try to remember what we have said!

EXERCISES

That annoying "tip of the tongue" problem happens to all of us. You meet someone very familiar, whom you are absolutely sure you know, but you can't remember either the name or the context in which you know them. Often it turns out to be your banker, but equally often it turns out to be somebody you really should remember.

One of the best memory techniques, for many people, is rhyme. You probably learned "Thirty days hath September . . ." as a young child. This same device helps with the names of people you meet.

Work at this in two steps. The first step is analyzing the person's face and features. This step is simple for most people. We can almost always tell that we have met someone before, even if we can't remember where, or when.

The second step is to repeat the name of the person. This gives you another clue. There's a technique called VAKT (Visual, Auditory, Kinaesthetic and Tactile) and these are the steps. When you repeat the name you hear it. Then, as soon as you can, write it down. Say it again, look at it again, and try to remember what it felt like when you wrote it.

Now make up a mnemonic rhyme, while the face and the name are fresh in your memory. For example, if you meet Jane Burke, you might try to rhyme it with "rain" and "work." As a bonus, make a mental picture of yourself working in the rain with Ms. Burke.

For practice, here are some totally new names—coined names—that you have never heard. Why absolutely strange names? Because in real life you'll be trying out this memory practice on totally new names. You have to practice learning something quite new, not something with which you are vaguely familiar.

Try the steps outlined previously. There's no face to associate, of course, but try remembering the name, saying it to yourself, writing it down, and then making up a rhyme.

George Rybino _____

_____

Willson Engold _____

_____

Max Rewbin _____

_____

Sallyie Kinge _____

_____

Karl Friye _____

_____

Several of these have no really suitable rhymes, but there are mental associations you could use. George Rybino, for example, might make you think of George Washington, and something like "why mean, oh?"

Willson Engold: A picture, in your mind, of Woodrow Wilson's face "in gold" (on a gold coin, for example).

Max Rewbin: You might think of a rhyme for this one: perhaps a saxophone (sax) in a shoe bin.

Sallyie Kinge: This might rhyme with a car rally with a crowned king judging the event.

Karl Friye: How about Karl with a K sitting on a griddle?

(If you think these examples overly ridiculous, we should point out that there is some psychological evidence to indicate that the sillier the association the more likely you are to remember it!)

Now for your review. Close this book, and try to recall the five names you just read and visualized. How many could you recall?

Now that you have reopened the book and seen the ones you missed, go back and make up your own associations, or rhymes, for them. Shut the book again, and see how many you can remember.

This time, if you could not remember the five names, the devices and memory aids you used were not satisfactory. We can't tell you which words to think of; we can only teach you a technique. You must adapt it to your own thought processes.

Remembering numbers is trickier. Evidence shows that we can't remember more than seven numbers at once. That is why many of us had trouble when the telephone numbers were digitalized. Many clever Mensans have helped to solve the problem for themselves and their friends by making up words and using them instead of numbers. For example, Roger Herz, of New York City Mensa, has been particularly ingenious in this regard. He has used such mnemonics as CUTE and then 3 numbers, ABCISSA, and various forms of words pertaining to bicycles, one of his hobbies. Another couple in a local Mensa group used DAY-NITE for their code, and Lee Werbin, formerly a local officer in New Jersey used SOFT 1 HA! as her former number. What can you do with your telephone number to make it easier for others to remember? Is there a telephone number you must call frequently but cannot remember? Can you make up a word with the letters on the dial or push buttons? Play with the letters or numbers and try to compose something catchy and memorable. Such playful mnemonics are probably the best single way of remembering telephone numbers.

The same idea, of course, will work for zip codes, with each number standing for a letter in the alphabet—or each pair of numbers, if you can work it out that way. For example, 26 could be either BF or Z.

Zero might present a problem here, but you can, and probably should, use the letter O for zero. The zip 07407, for example, would be OGDOG, and that is probably a lot easier to remember than

07407, especially with a mental picture of OG with his DOG as an aide-mémoire.

Create mnemonic devices of these sample zip codes to help you remember them.

09456 _____

08540 _____

10032 _____

10105 _____

97635 _____

Now that you have tried those, how about the nine-digit codes that theoretically are impossible to remember? Here are some fictitious codes; you can make up words for both parts, for either one, or in any combination that you feel would help you to remember. Try various combinations and see which type helps you to remember better.

909456-9090 _____

10023-4567 _____

73456-6262 _____

89430-7601 _____

45419-3798 _____

Which method worked better for you?

Scientists have their own ways of memorizing. There are dozens of sentences medical students use for memorizing the nerves. One famous one runs: "On old Olympus' Lofty Tops a Greek and German brewed some hops." According to Martin Gardner, in *Mathematical Puzzles and Diversions,* this dates back to 1634, when Pierre Herigone published a system for using consonants for digits. Then he suggested adding vowels to make words, and memorizing the words by methods that were well known even then. Gardner points out that if you memorize a long chain of numbers, the mental pictures tend to fade very quickly, unless you have memorized the entire list.

A method often taught for such things as remembering pi utilizes a sentence in which the number of letters in each word corresponds to each number you wish to remember. For example, if you want to remember 3.1416, a sentence might read "And, I want a banana." That is 3 letters, 1 letter, 4 letters, 1 letter, and 6 letters. This is most likely to work if you make the sentence significant to yourself. (A member of Swiss Mensa once gave the extended numbers of pi up to several thousand, which he had memorized.)

Are there phone numbers you wish to memorize that cannot be turned into words? Is there an address you keep forgetting? Write them down here:

1. _____

2. _____

3. _____

Now make up a sentence in which each numeral is represented by a word with the same number of letters. If the number is 143, you could memorize "I work yet." If it happened to be the address of Joe Jones, you might make up a sentence like "I know Joe." This would have the double advantage of reminding you that it is Joe's number, and of fixing the number firmly in your mind in association with Joe. Try it for the three sets of numbers you have listed above:

1. _____

2. _____

3. _____

MEMORY EXAM

1. What are the following phone numbers? (Don't look them up, naturally!)

   a. Your doctor _____

   b. Your local police department (outside those areas where it is 999) _____

   c. Your maintenance or custodial person (where applicable) _____

   d. Your plumber (again, where applicable) _____

e. Your stockbroker, or your bank, or wherever you call most often about your financial business

_____

Obviously, we can't give you the answers for these, but if you don't know the answers immediately, use some of the techniques reviewed in this chapter. Just think of the time you will save not having to look up that number!

For the following quotes, dates, and names of famous people—some of which are wrong, some of which are right—check "Right" or "Wrong." If you check "Wrong," see if you can correct the error. That should be a spur to improve your memory.

1. "Water, water, everywhere/And not a drop to drink."

   Right: _____ Wrong: _____ Correction: _____

2. The famous philosopher John Stuart Mills

   Right: _____ Wrong: _____ Correction: _____

3. "Money is the root of all evil."

   Right: _____ Wrong: _____ Correction: _____

4. Harry Spencer Truman

   Right: _____ Wrong: _____ Correction: _____

5. "Spare the rod and spoil the child."—Proverbs 13:24

   Right: _____ Wrong: _____ Correction: _____

6. "Who steals my purse steals trash."

   Right: _____ Wrong: _____ Correction: _____

7. The Declaration of Independence was signed on July 4, 1776.

   Right: _____ Wrong: _____ Correction: _____

8. "Candy/Is dandy/But liquor/Is quicker." —Dorothy Parker

   Right: _____ Wrong: _____ Correction: _____

9. "Go west, young man." —Horace Greeley.

   Right: _____ Wrong: _____ Correction: _____

10. Samson lost his strength when Delilah cut (or shaved) his hair.

   Right: _____ Wrong: _____ Correction: _____

11. William the Conqueror defeated Harold at Hastings, England, in 1066.

Right: _____ Wrong: _____ Correction: _____

12. Ignace Paderewski was a premier of Poland.

Right: _____ Wrong: _____ Correction: _____

13. The Man in the Iron Mask was a twin brother of King Louis XIV of France.

Right: _____ Wrong: _____ Correction: _____

14. Henry VIII was a contemporary of Christopher Columbus.

Right: _____ Wrong: _____ Correction: _____

15. Lizzie Borden, of Fall River, Massachusetts, is notorious in American history for having murdered her father and step-mother with an ax.

Right: _____ Wrong: _____ Correction: _____

ANSWERS

1. *Wrong.* The exact quote is "Nor any drop to drink." ("The Rhyme of the Ancient Mariner," by Samuel Taylor Coleridge)

2. *Wrong.* His name is John Stuart Mill.

3. *Wrong.* The quote runs "The love of money is the root of all evil" (1 Timothy 6:10).

4. *Wrong.* Harry S. Truman had no middle name, and preferably no middle initial.

5. *Wrong.* "He that spareth his rod hateth his son" (Proverbs 13:24).

6. *Right.* Said by Shakespeare (*Othello* 3:3), as often happens.

7. *Wrong.* The final draft was drawn up and concluded that day. The signing was spread out over a long period of time.

8. *Wrong.* Ogden Nash penned *those* immortal words.

9. *Wrong.* Greeley quoted it, but it was written by John Soule, and Greeley gave him credit. (Incidentally, west at that time was Ohio.)

10. *Wrong.* Delilah called for a man to come and shave off Samson's "seven locks" (Judges 16:19).

11. *Wrong.* The defeat occurred at a spot called Battle, where Battle Abbey is now located.

12. *Right.* He was, in 1919.

13. *Wrong.* There is no good evidence that he was.

14. *Right.* Their life spans overlapped by about fifteen years.

15. *Wrong.* Despite the folklore about her, Lizzie Borden was acquitted. She may be notorious for being considered guilty, but legally she was found not guilty.

How well did you do on this memory quiz? If not too well, the next time you think you remember something, go back and check up on it. Part of thinking smart is verifying what you know—or don't know.

6

ARE YOU GRAMMAR SMART?

Struck by the frequent grammatical errors that appear in even the most erudite materials, we have kept track of such slips for more than a year. To our surprise, a small number of errors accounted for almost all the mistakes. Put another way, only a few words, phrases or expressions really grate on the ear and offend the eye. They also spoil any "smart" image you may want to project, as truly smart people know the difference.

Since we can't think of anyone who enjoys drills and repetition, we came up with something different, a mystery story. The following tale contains a fair number of grammatical errors. Underline the mistakes you find or mark them on a separate sheet of paper, and try to supply the correct alternative in each case. Then, when you have finished, check our list at the end and compare. Incidentally, you should be able to solve the mystery en route to grammatical perfection.

THE MYSTERY OF THE MURDERED MAID

That brave and famous detective Mr. Bare Bones strolled home on a balmy evening in the early 1920s. The twenties had not yet started to roar, and the atmosphere was calm and peaceful. His friend Dr. Fatsome was waiting for him in his pleasant living room. "Ah, my dear friend," said the detective, tossing his hat on the floor, "I'm delighted to see you. But what brings you here in such a hurry that you weren't able to call me first, but took the chance of dropping in? No matter. As far as I'm concerned, for you and I to be together again is a real pleasure, regardless of the reason."

The good doctor nodded and smiled. "I'm glad to see you too, but it really is not a pleasant business." He continued, "I've just had a phone call from the Countess. Her former maid, who retired some ten years ago, was supposed to come to stay for a week, as a surprise to one of the guests. She never arrived. The most puzzling feature of the disappearance is it's unexpectedness. The old woman telephoned in the morning to say she was leaving immediately and would take a taxi to the castle and arrive by noon; but she never showed up."

Bones looked concerned. "Have they called in the police?"

The doctor shook his head. "I asked about that, and the Countess said that even though she was afraid the poor old lady would be found laying in a ditch somewhere, she didn't want to frighten her unduly if she had just had a loss of memory, or something like that. She wants us to track down the woman, if we can, without alarming her."

"The game's afoot," gloated the detective. "We're on our way."

In less than two hours they had reached the castle. There they found the Countess and her houseguest, Colonel Smithly-Cholomondley-Prowse (pronounced, obviously, Schump). Neither of the two was adverse to discussing the disappearance in fulsome detail.

The Countess began the story. "The Colonel is the son of two of my dearest friends. Years ago, they all stayed here for six months, before they went out to live in Australia. Last year I had a lovely letter from the Colonel, saying that they had both died and he was returning to England. Unfortunately, the ship ran into a typhoon on the way and was wrecked. Most, but not all, of the passengers were saved, but my dear friends' son was most happily spared, and he finally reached England only last week. As a special surprise, and without telling him, I had invited my retired maid, who had taken care of him forty years ago, when he was only seven or eight. I was sure she would enjoy meeting him again and reminiscing. She's the example of what an old nurse should be. She was the nurse for my children before she became my personal maid. My youngsters are all over the world now, unfortunately, but she would be the Colonel's link with the past."

The Colonel twirled his mustache as he spoke. He looked very sad. "Terrible thing, this disappearance. I was very fond of old Martha, you know. Even though she flaunted all the rules for nursemaids, she was very good to me when I was here, and spoiled me outrageously."

The great detective began his questioning. "What happened in the shipwreck?"

"Oh, it was really not much, except for my poor roommate," said the Colonel rather lightly. "We were wrecked about a week after we left Australia. Only three people were killed, including the poor chap I was sharing a room with. The rest of us were picked up, one way or another, by different ships. I was the only one taken aboard an American ship going through the Panama Canal, and I came home the long way."

"Did you enjoy the extra weeks at sea once you got over your sadness about the shipwreck?"

"One of the finest voyages of my life," said the Colonel. "I'll never forget being out on deck very early one morning as we went through the canal. I watched us steam into the sunrise! Absolutely magnificent—wonderful engineering feat."

The conversation continued briefly, and then Bones said to the Countess, "I'm very much afraid there's been some foul play here. My friend and myself are going to search the immediate neighborhood and report back."

Not an hour later, the two men found the body of the elderly maid hidden in the woods behind the house, in a shallow grave. They returned to the castle soberly, and called in the Colonel and the Countess again.

"I do not recall your saying why you had returned to England at this particular time," the detective inquired of the Colonel.

"My parents died about a year ago. They were both only children, I have no cousins, and the famous Smithly-Cholomondley-Prowse diamonds are safely tucked away here. I'd like to sell off a few and enlarge our place in Australia."

The detective reached out and grabbed the Colonel. "Countess, call the police instantly. This man is not only an impostor, he's a murderer. He won't be able to plead innocent to this charge."

Later, after the local police had removed the Colonel, who had collapsed, Dr. Fatsome pressed Bones for an explanation. "You owe both me and the Countess the complete story," he said.

"I'll tell the two of you, but let him wrack his brain in prison over the mistake he made," said the great detective. "The Colonel wasn't even on the ship, I'm sure. Your poor friend, the real Smithly-Cholomondley-Prowse, either drowned during the shipwreck or was murdered by his roommate. That roommate must have teamed up with the man passing himself off as your friend. The real Smithly-Cholomondley-Prowse had undoubtedly told the whole story of his inheritance to the roommate, who survived—somehow—and who got in touch with this impostor. I'm sure the real chap's roommate will turn out to be the wrong age—or have the wrong accent, or something of the sort. Since he could not do it, he found someone with the proper accent, and the right degree of villainy, to impersonate the missing heir. All was going well until this well-coached impersonator overheard the Countess talking to the maid this morning on the telephone. He realized that the old family retainer would spot him instantly as an impostor, so he sneaked out of the house, waylaid her as she got out of the taxi, and murdered her. I'm sure they'll get his accomplice, the roommate, also."

Bones was correct, as usual. When confronted with the evidence, the accomplice confessed, plus he incriminated a fence who was going to sell the jewels.

Now, can you figure out the two problems that Bones solved? The first is to determine what slip the "Colonel" made that gave him away so completely. The second task, which may be easier or harder, depending on you, is to find and explain the ten errors that were perpetrated during the course of the story. The answers to the ten not-smarts follow:

1. *for you and I to be together* . . . This is the old "I" vs. "me" argument. Would you ever say, "This is a real pleasure for I?" No, you certainly would not. When in doubt as to whether to use "I" or "me," ask yourself one question—what would I say if I were talking about myself? The answer to that question is the correct usage.

2. *it's unexpectedness* . . . The apostrophe means that "it is" has been shortened to "it's." And, of course, that is not what is meant in this case.

3. *found laying in a ditch* . . . This should be "lying." The problem arises because there are two different words, both of them spelled "lay." Unfortunately, the present tense of the verb "lay" and the past tense of the verb "lie" are both "lay." The old children's prayer would be a good memory help. The prayer says, "Now I lay me down to sleep." That "lay me" is the clue. The child is laying himself down. That you don't lie bricks, you lay them, is another clue. "Lie" on the other hand, is the present of "lie." So, today you lie down on your beach towel, and you were lying on your beach towel yesterday, but you lay bricks today and you laid bricks yesterday.

4. *was adverse* . . . This particular error crops up in many places, and seems to be one of the most common mistakes. "Adverse" comes from the same root as "adversary" and has the meaning of hostility or fighting. "Averse," on the other hand, means reluctant. When you have an aversion to something, you aren't fighting it; you just don't like it. Or how about a mental picture of averting an accident by turning away—there is no hostility involved.

5. *fulsome* . . . According to most (but not all) dictionaries, this does not mean full of; it means insincere, or offensive, which was not the sense it was used in the example given. (We must point out, in all fairness, that an occasional dictionary allows this use, but careful writers won't. Why risk it when you can use a word properly?)

6. *she flaunted all the rules* . . . "Flaunt" and "flout" have two entirely different meanings. While "flout" is almost never used for "flaunt," "flaunt" is all too often used for "flout." Some rather permissive dictionaries have included both meanings under "flaunt," but this destroys a perfectly good word and there is almost nothing to take its place. For want of a better mnemonic, "flout" means to be with*out* the rules, or *out*side the rules. To show off, or display proudly, is "flaunt." Since the nursemaid was breaking the rules, she was flouting them. (If you feel you need a mnemonic for "flaunt," besides the fact that it isn't flout, you might think of *Aunt*ie Mame, who really flaunted it.)

7. *My friend and myself* . . . Would you say, "Myself is going to search the neighborhood"? The misuse of the pronouns "myself," "himself," "herself," etc. is all too common.

8. *plead innocent* . . . The burden of proof is always on the prosecution, not the defense or the defendant. Anyone who is arrested does not have to prove he is innocent; the prosecution has to prove he is guilty. There is a tremendous difference, especially to the person who is arrested. In the United States (and most countries where the laws originated in British law) but not in France, the person who has been charged pleads guilty, or not guilty. The verdict is always delivered in that form: Guilty, or Not Guilty. (We won't discuss exceptions like the "Not Proven" that shows up once in a while in Scotland.)

9. *wrack his brain* . . . This is purely a written grammatical error. Orally, there is no *w* when you rack your brain, nor even if you incorrectly "wrack" it. Here's the distinction: "wrack" comes from "wreck," and involves total destruction. If pain-racked or guilt-racked, you are only being tortured—as if you were on a rack—but not destroyed, usually.

10. *plus he incriminated* . . . "Plus" does not mean "and furthermore." It doesn't even mean "as a bonus." Yet it is used that way in far too many instances. One of the more popular words of the decade, it is in most instances used incorrectly. The literal meaning is "with the addition of," and that is the only meaning that traditionalists accept as correct. Substitute the words "with the addition of" wherever you see or hear "plus," and you will see the error. Make the substitution in the story, and you have: "with the addition of, he incriminated a fence." That's obviously not correct.

How did you do? Did you get 8 or more errors? Did you spot them all? If not, list whatever you missed, and work to correct your grammatical misconceptions.

And now for the grand denouement you have eagerly awaited. How did our famous detective realize that the elegant "Colonel" was an impostor, and had not even been on that ill-fated ship? If you know your geography, this is easy. When you sail from Australia to England via the Panama Canal, obviously you go from the Pacific to the Atlantic ocean. Equally obviously, the Pacific is west of the Atlantic, so you would certainly see a sunrise in the east as you traversed the canal, wouldn't you? Well, thanks to an odd bend in the Isthmus of Panama, you sail *east to west* when you go from the Pacific to the Atlantic! This defies common sense, but matches the geographical reality, and everyone who transits the Panama Canal is informed of this peculiarity. Ergo, the ''Colonel'' was an impostor, who had never sailed through the canal. (Our detective was unsure whether the Colonel had been the real heir's roommate, or whether the roommate had sought him out. It did turn out that the Colonel had roomed with the true heir, and had thus learned enough to pass himself off as the inheritor of the family jewelry. It also turned out that the false Colonel had murdered the real hyphenated heir, as well as the nursemaid!) It was also obvious the Colonel had arrived via Suez.

GRAMMARAMA

Now try the following games to see how you have improved your grammatical skills. You'll need, in addition, to sharpen your poetry skills, your cryptogram skills, and your thinking skills.

TEST

1. The following limerick will rhyme and scan only if you insert the correct words.

> A clever young fellow who thought
> That grammar could never be taught
> Said, ''Between you and _____
> _____ all nonsense, you see,
> And __ __ I've never been caught.

2. The following limerick won't work if you use the wrong grammar:

My hen and dog follow the rule
Though neither has yet been to school

| 13 25 | 4 15 7 | 12 9 5 19 | 1 20 | 13 25 | 6 5 5 20 |
| 13 25 | 8 5 14 | 12 1 25 19 | 5 7 7 19 | 20 15 | 5 1 20 |

And neither one lays in the pool.

3. The following word square has a coiled ending which will complete a rhyme. One of the authors has coined the name Terse Verse for this form of puzzle, where the first line or more start a rhyme, and the puzzle or cryptogram finishes it. Move one letter at a time, in any direction. (X's are nulls.)

I'm averse to adverse for dislike; it is wrong

A	I	N	R	O
N	N	P	E	S
D	A	O	O	R
V	T	I	I	N
E	R	I	S	X
S	E	D	O	X
C	O	N	N	G

4. In the following paragraph, take the number of incorrect apostrophes, add the number of other grammatical errors you can find, and divide by two. See if your answer matches ours:

"It's a pity," said the young man. "I think this idea is worth it's weight in gold. Plus, of course, I'm working on another idea right now that will make you and I a fortune, if it's a success. I hope that you and your wife, and my wife and myself, will be rolling in money this time next year. I really intend to work hard on this and flaunt all the usual rules for making money. It's not as if I didn't have a good business training. Between you and I, my professors at the business school were absolutely brilliant. They gave me one idea that is so brilliant in it's conception that if I can ever work it out, I'll make a million. I'm not adverse to accepting good ideas, especially when it's an idea like this. It's so clever in it's concept that it should succeed. I really must give some credit to my wife, though—some of the work is her's.''

5.   While this may not be grammar, strictly speaking, can you figure out any way to write the following sentence, which is obviously not correct: *There are three ways to write two in words.*

ANSWERS

1. A clever young fellow who thought
   That grammar could never be taught
   Said, "Between you and *me*,
   It's all nonsense, you see,
   And *what's more*, I've never been caught."

   You could have had a number of different words on the last line, but "plus" would leave you short one syllable, compared with the first two lines, not to mention its flouting of grammatical rules.

2. My hen and dog follow the rule
   Though neither has yet been to school.
   My dog lies at my feet,
   My hen lays eggs to eat
   And neither one lays in the pool!

3. If you start at the upper left, with the A, you will find that the second line says:
   AN ADVERSE CONDITION IN PROSE OR IN SONG.

4. The answer is 5.

5. The three homonyms are "two," "too," and "to." If you figure out a way to render this idea, please let us know.

7

THE LOGIC OF LOGIC

As a branch of philosophy, logic may sound a bit arcane or intimidating (it is neither), but as a tool for living—well, we simply couldn't function without it. Logic lies at the heart of even our simplest everyday decisions, such as how to balance the family budget or keep our files in order. It can help us solve a puzzle for fun or a real-life dilemma, and show us how to "keep our heads" in a quarrel or reach a compromise. It can help us decide that one product is superior to another, that plan A is more feasible than plan B. It can help us choose between two candidates for public office and follow their lines of reasoning. Most important, it allows us to convey our own ideas with clarity, to weigh others' arguments carefully or persuade them to see things our way. In short, by training our minds to think more logically, we can manage more successfully at home, at school, as citizens, or on the job.

John Stuart Mill, whose estimated 192 IQ would certainly have qualified him for membership in Mensa (assuming that IQ points then were qualitatively the same as they are today), defined logic as "the science of reasoning, as well as an art founded on that science." But like most other scientific terms in popular use, it can have a number of different meanings. For example, "logic" may describe the act of drawing conclusions from two premises or basic assumptions, usually called a syllogism; it may also mean deriving "particulars" from a general statement.

Aristotle asked that the art of argumentation also be included under the heading of logic. And still others have called logic "structured reasoning"—"structure" being the key word.

To begin with syllogisms, here is an example:

Mensans have high IQs.
George the pig has a high IQ.
Therefore George the pig must be a member of Mensa.

Didn't George Orwell say, "Some pigs are more equal than other pigs"?

Logic also deals with Venn diagrams, those three-ring constructs that remind one of the old three-ring Ballantine sign. They have to do with class relationships and helping us sort them out. Without Venn diagrams you might not know what class you belong to—which could get you in trouble at school, at the club, or in any Marxist society.

In this logic chapter we will also consider paradoxes, such as the ouroboros, and the Möbius strip. We will learn about the conditions that must be present for a logical paradox to occur, and we will finally get into the fable of the truthtellers and the liars. Is there really an island that contains only truthtellers and liars? And if so, do they have white or black spots on their foreheads? Knowing the answers should help you separate truth from lies in real life and correct any misleading statement you come across.

Finally, it is clear that we cannot give you a course on logic in the space of this small chapter, but we can give you a small chapter in this course on logic, and, perhaps, teach you to think a little smarter in the process.

THE PARADOX OF LOGIC*

Consider this:

You come to a ravine over which there is a deep bridge that looks extremely unsafe. There are three men across the ravine, and you know that only liars and truthtellers live in this country. You want to be sure the bridge is safe, and you want to ask a truthteller. You shout to one man, "Are you a truthteller?" You can't hear the first man, A, but man B says, "He said he was a truthteller." Man C shouts across, "No he didn't, he said he was a liar." Which one was telling the truth?

This paradox can be worked out quite easily. You could not hear man A. However, if he was a liar, he would have said that he was a truthteller (a lie); and if he was a truthteller, he would have had to say so (the truth). Therefore, no matter what, he would have said he was a truthteller. Obviously, therefore, man B told the truth, and man C did not. You had better ask man B whether the bridge is safe.

Paradoxes are based on a set of self-contradictory statements that derive from logical reasoning and at first appear to be true. There is the story of the man who was told: "You have been sentenced to death some weekday next week, but you will not know on what day we have scheduled your execution until you are awakened in the morning." The prisoner proved to his satisfaction that it could not be Friday, because if he hadn't been executed by then, he would know Friday was the fatal day. If you carry this through, you will see that he could reasonably conclude he couldn't be executed any day. Unfortunately the authorities didn't see it that way and chose Monday.

---

* If you like this chapter, we suggest devouring the works of Raymond Smullyan, who has written extensively on the subject. One of his titles is *What Is the Name of This Book?*

The classic paradox is the card that says on one side: "The sentence on the other side of this card is true." The reverse says: "The sentence on the other side of this card is false." Each statement can be true by itself, but not in conjunction with the other.

A Möbius strip is a visual paradox. Visual paradoxes have a long and venerable history. If you look at the illustration of a Möbius strip, here are two puzzles you might be able to solve.

1. If you start at one point on a Möbius strip and draw a line completely around the strip until it meets the beginning, what side of the paper will it be on?
2. If you take a pair of scissors and cut a Möbius strip with an additional half turn right down the middle of the paper, what will you have?

to visualize, but is a kind of Möbius strip in three dimensions. It is not only one-sided but it has no edges.

The ouroboros, the snake with his tail in his mouth, is the prototype of the "vicious circle."

The Möbius strip is another example of vicious circularity, or visual contradiction. You can make one yourself by taking a strip of paper, giving it half a twist, and then sticking the ends of the paper together. Follow its edge. You will find it has only one side.

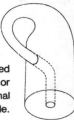

The Klein bottle is a closed surface with no inside or outside—a three-dimensional "bottle" with only one side.

ANSWERS

1. You will find that although you did not turn the paper, the line you have drawn is both inside and outside, on both sides of the paper.
2. You will find you have two interlocking rings, not two separate circles.

Try this paradox about the universal solvent—the material that dissolves everything: An alchemist, revealing that he had found what the king was looking for, the universal solvent, announced he would bring it to the royal presence. Yet when he showed up with a liquid in a beautiful container, the king has him arrested. Why? This particular problem is both a paradox and a contradiction: If the alchemist really had the universal solvent, in what could it be contained?

Take the well-known land of the liars and the truthtellers again. One of the inhabitants tells a visitor who is standing next to two, and only two, inhabitants, "There is at least one liar here." Is the speaker a liar or a truthteller? Let's look at it logically: If he were a liar, he could not make that statement, because it would be true. Therefore he would have to be a truthteller. And since a truthteller cannot also be a liar, the other man must be a liar.

The Terrible Smith, Jones, Robinson Problem

What is probably the most famous of all such puzzles, which has appeared in numerous books, is the famous (or infamous) Smith, Jones, Robinson problem.

This type of problem runs as follows: A train runs between New York and Chicago. The brakeman, the engineer, and the fireman, are named Smith, Jones, and Robinson, not necessarily in that order. The three passengers are Mr. Smith, Mr. Jones and Mr. Robinson. Mr. Robinson lives in New York. The brakeman lives halfway between New York and Chicago. Mr. Jones earns exactly $20,000 a year. Smith beat the fireman at cards. The brakeman's next-door neighbor, who is a passenger on this train, earns exactly three times as much as the brakeman. The passenger who lives in Chicago has the same name as the brakeman. What is the name of the engineer?

You can list the conditions given in the story:

a. Mr. Robinson lives in New York.
b. The brakeman lives halfway between New York and Chicago.
c. Mr. Jones earns exactly $20,000 per year.
d. Smith beat the fireman at cards.
e. The brakeman's next-door neighbor, who is a passenger, earns exactly three times the brakeman's salary.
f. The passenger who lives in Chicago has the same name as the brakeman.

Taking these facts in order, we see that according to *f*, Smith cannot be the fireman. According to *b*, the brakeman's neighbor cannot be Mr. Robinson. He can't be Mr. Jones either, because you cannot divide $20,000 (*c*) by three exactly (*e*). Because Mr. Robinson lives in New York (*a*), the brakeman's neighbor must be Mr. Smith, as we have ruled out the other two. Thus Mr. Smith lives halfway between New York and Chicago (*b*); and since Mr. Robinson lives in New York, only Mr. Jones is left to live in Chicago. So according to *f*, the brakeman is Jones. We have now ruled out the fireman and the brakeman, leaving Smith as the engineer.

Many Mensans like these logic puzzles, but many are intimidated by them. Several years ago, Rick Trilling, of Framingham, Massachusetts, devised an excellent method for solving them (*Mensa Bulletin*, April 1979).

You can solve these puzzles by using a chart (see example on p. 64). This matrix form allows each fact in each category to be placed at an intersection where it will interact with each of the other categories. In the example given of Smith, Jones,

	Brakeman	Fireman	Engineer
Robinson		X	
Jones	X		
Smith			X

and Robinson, each fact given could be entered on such a chart. When you label such a chart properly, for all possible facts about each person or item you are considering, you then enter each fact (or "clue") on the chart. If you have two items from different sets of clues that you can be sure do not equal each other, you enter an X in the box where the two clues intersect. After you have finished entering all the clues, each blank square at an intersection presents a truth, or gives you correct information. In the previous example, for instance, the brakeman's neighbor could not be Robinson or Jones. By a process of elimination, he had to be Mr. Smith. If you work out the Smith, Jones, Robinson problem on a matrix like the one above, you will have a clear, understandable visual model of how this method works. You should place the names across the top of the box matrix you will need, and the occupations down the left, as in the example.

The practical value of this type of puzzle is that it conditions you to think through a problem logically, draw inferences, and reach verifiable conclusions. The latter skill, especially, is not always available to those who draw inferences, which may be why so many incorrect inferences are drawn.

Try this logic puzzle, using the matrix on page 65. Every time you are given a fact, put a check mark in each and every box that can be shown to be true, and an X in each that is not true. That should give you the correct solution. (See page 72 for answer.)

		This Week					Last Week				
		1	2	3	4	5	1	2	3	4	5
	Austen										
	Beckett										
	Cather										
	Dostoevsky										
	Egan										
Last Week	First										
	Second										
	Third										
	Fourth										
	Fifth										

Five friends—Austen, Beckett, Cather, Dostoevsky, and Egan—all wrote novels, and all are selling very well. Dostoevsky's novel did better this week than Egan's, but not as well as the novel that was fourth on the best-seller list. However, not one of these was first on the list this week. Last week, Cather's novel sold better than the novel that was fifth this week. However, the novel that was fifth this week sold better last week than the novel that was second on the best-seller list this week, but none of these was at the bottom last week. Austen's novel didn't do as well this week as Beckett's. It did, however, perform better than the novel that was fifth last week. The novel that was second this week was not fourth last week.

By one definition, logic is the process of drawing a conclusion from two statements or propositions, called premises. If you start from a false premise, it is possible to have a set of logical conclusions that are totally false. That is what many people do not understand. There is a confusion between logical reasoning and truth. Not everything that is logical is also true. We can prove that cats are dogs, just as, earlier, we proved that a pig can have a high IQ. The reasoning can be entirely logical, but if the original premise, or any succeeding premise, is not true, the conclusion may not be true. What we are discussing here, of course, is only the branch of logic known as formal logic, and only one small area of that, syllogisms.

A standard categorical syllogism will have three terms. The first is the major premise—the first sentence, which tells the major term. The second term is the minor premise, and the last term is the conclusion.

Why bother with syllogisms? To prove that all dogs are cats really won't help you, because obviously that is not true—a fallacy we will talk about later. But it will help you a great deal to be able to work out a syllogism when somebody is trying to sell you something, or persuade you of something, or argue with you on a logical basis.

If you follow through the chapter, and learn how to do syllogisms, you can reason your way through arguments. You can, for example, counter family arguments, sales pitches, political arguments, and business propositions, in a manner that is logical and effective.

You can learn to counter the argument: "The Jones Company leased out its payroll and just look at its profit-and-loss statement. We should do the same."

If you're advised that everybody enjoys a vacation at Club X and therefore you will too, a simple syllogism may (note: we do not say *will*) convince your adviser that you are not necessarily everybody, in the first place, and that the statement that everybody likes Club X may or may not be true.

You can also discuss your purchase of a new car with the

seller more confidently. When you become used to syllogisms, you will be able to construct one in your mind, and point out flaws in the argument that because the Droshky is the best-selling auto in the United States, you should buy one too.

Here's a valid syllogism:

All A is B.
All C is A.
Therefore all C is B.

You have included all C in the category A, and all category A is B. Therefore, all category C is B also.

You will find that all arguments constructed on this basis, if followed exactly, are correct. For example:

All apples are fruits.
All Golden Delicious are apples.
Therefore all Golden Delicious are fruits.

On the other hand, there are forms of syllogism that are inaccurate. We can take the same sort of information given above and make a syllogism that says:

All A is B.
Some C is A.
Therefore all C is B.

You can see by looking at this syllogism that you have not allowed for the implicit fact that some C is not A. Unfortunately, when this argument is put into words, it sometimes sounds right; as in:

All painters are artists.
Some members of the general public are artists.
Therefore some members of the general public are painters.

It is incorrect, regardless of whether the last statement is true or not, because of the form. This can be demonstrated by choosing absurdities as the statements.

All airplanes fly.
Some birds fly.
Therefore some birds are airplanes.

As a think-smart technique for demolishing illogical arguments, that cannot be bettered. When you find somebody arguing incorrectly, as in this last illogical syllogism, simply reply: "According to those rules, what you are saying is: All cats eat fish; some dogs eat fish; therefore some dogs are cats."

This is a good way to fight propaganda that you know is incorrect. When someone argues based on such an incorrect syllogism, check the pattern. If the second line uses the word "some" and then proceeds to a conclusion that depends on the "all" of the first assumption, analyze the syllogism for yourself. Come up with a silly conclusion, such as that some dogs are cats, and you are safe in challenging the conclusion!

Solve this one: All glorps are purple; some snoofs are purple; therefore some snoofs are glorps. True or false?

False, according to the syllogism.

This testing of a syllogism is also useful for checking up on such things as advertising claims.

All women want to be beautiful.
These movie stars are beautiful and use Gloppo.
Therefore you will be beautiful if you use Gloppo.

If you analyze this, you will see that it falls into the category that proves some dogs are cats.

Another technique for testing syllogisms is the Venn diagram, a valuable tool for people whose thinking tends to be visual. Three overlapping circles are labeled with terms from a syllogism. Here's a nonsense example:

Some worples are purple; some glorps are purple; therefore some worples are glorps.

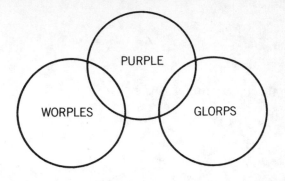

As you can easily see from the picture, you cannot draw the last conclusion from the premises. It's *possible* that some worples are glorps, but not *necessarily* true.

Here's another type of syllogism that can be shown in a diagram:

All cats are mammals.
All dogs are mammals.
Therefore all cats are dogs.

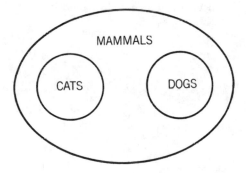

This shows graphically that there is nothing in the syllogism that necessitates cats being dogs.

Now try this one:

All A is C.
All B is A.
Therefore, all B is C.

The logical diagram for this syllogism is different.

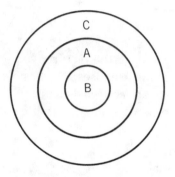

This diagram shows clearly that there is an overlap. (This is not, as drawn, a Venn diagram, because it reflects "all" statements, not "some" statements.)

THE TEST OF LOGIC

For each of the following syllogisms, prove whether it is valid or invalid, either by setting up a nonsense syllogism or by drawing a Venn diagram.

1. All glorps are snorkels.
   All whiffles are glorps.
   Therefore all whiffles are snorkels.

2. All newspapers are read.
   All magazines are read.
   Therefore all magazines are newspapers.

3. All countries on the equator are hot.
   Ecuador is on the equator.
   Therefore Ecuador is hot.

4. All beggars are poor.
   All glorps are poor.
   Therefore all glorps are beggars.

5. All birds fly.
   A kiwi bird is a bird.
   Therefore a kiwi bird flies.

6. All Republicrats are reactionaries.
   John Jones is a Republicrat.
   Therefore John Jones is a reactionary.

You can translate that first sentence to: "Women are bad drivers," and conclude from it that a woman caused a particular accident. You can reverse the argument and state: "All men are sexist." That can provide a logically correct argument if the proper premises and qualifications are added, but it is based on a generalization that cannot be demonstrated to be universally true. So, technically, you can win the argument by pointing this out—i.e., that the statement "All men are sexist" is not a demonstrable fact—especially if you can show one man who is not. We would not like to bet on the outcome of the argument, however, since even the most logical argument often fails against emotion.

ANSWERS

1. *All whiffles are snorkels.* Yes, this is logical, no matter which method you use.

2. *All magazines are newspapers.* No, this is not logical, no matter which method you use, as there is no connection to show the two are equal.

3. *Ecuador is hot.* Yes, this is logical. It would also have been logical if it had said that all countries on the equator are cold. Based on a false premise, it would have been logically correct but untrue.

4. *All glorps are beggars.* No, this isn't logical, for the same reason as number 2, above.

5. *A kiwi bird flies.* This is a correct syllogism, but it is not true. A kiwi bird does not fly. It should be obvious from this example that if you start with a false premise, your argument may be perfectly logical but the conclusion, while logical, can be untrue. This is the sticking point for many people who basically understand how to reason logically. If they argue logically, they conclude, then their answers must be true.

6. *John Jones is a reactionary.* Obviously, this is true only if the first premise can be shown to be true. This particular technique can be hard to fight against, whether it is a political argument or a family fight. (You are always late for a party; there is a party tonight for you; therefore you will be late for the party.)

The matrix problem on page 65 is slightly more difficult. However, it can be solved by the method shown. Dostoevsky's novel wasn't fifth this week, nor was Austen's, nor Beckett's, nor Cather's. If you cross out all of those—clues 1, 2, and 3—you will be left with the only possible conclusion: Egan was fifth. Now we go on to last week: Clues 2 and 3 tell us that it was not Austen, Beckett, Cather, or Egan who ranked fifth, so you can cross those out. Therefore it had to be Dostoevsky. If you mark on the chart all the facts given, in exactly the same manner, you will find that, logically, last week will rank Cather, Egan, Beckett, Austen, and Dostoevsky; this week will rank Cather, Beckett, Austen, Dostoevsky, and Egan. If you missed any of these, go back and check the clues to see where you made your error.

So now you know how to think logically? Try it out on various problems, in life situations, and on puzzles. (We have some here.) See if you have learned something about thinking straight.

In the back of the book, in the test and review chapter, "What Have You Learned?," you will find some advertising, some syllogisms, and some statements. We will ask you, with what you have learned, to draw conclusions, to analyze the logic used, and to determine whether or not the material is logical. All of that is well and good, but don't forget that if you start from a premise that is not true, all the logic in the world won't make the conclusion necessarily true. If you start with the premise that the moon is made of green cheese, and argue logically, you can prove a great many things logically. But it doesn't mean that the moon is indeed made of green cheese!

Still another form of logical thinking, not really specifically related to the preceding discussion but very important nonetheless, is the matter of similarities and sequencing. Intelligence tests consider this form of logical thinking so important that all major tests include it. The various group tests like the Scholastic Aptitude Test (SAT), and the more advanced tests like those for admission to graduate schools, usually have a section on visual and verbal analogies. How do you use logic to figure out those puzzling sequences, or the analogous words?

SEQUENCES AND SIMILARITIES

One of the most useful forms of logical thinking is similarities and differences, which is also one of the most popular areas in tests. Unless you practice a very specific profession, or unless you are already at the top of your field, the chances are excellent that you will someday find yourself taking some sort of test—for further education, or for employment. Projections show that one person in three will have to switch careers or get further education at some time between twenty and fifty years of age. If you are one of those three, learning these methods of logical thinking may make all the difference between a high score and a low one.

For preparation or for fun, then, perhaps you would care to ask yourself: What should follow in this alphabetical sequence?

A   CD   GHI   MNOP

Let's analyze the series of letters. The most obvious pattern is one, two, three, four letters. You can fairly conclude that the next group will consist of five letters. But some letters have been omitted; what are they? If you look, you will see that one letter has been skipped after the first letter, two letters have been omitted after the two-letter group, and so on. Now you have the pattern. Omit four letters, and you will be left with the concluding sequence of five letters—UVWXY. Easy, wasn't it?

Not all sequential puzzles are that easy. Try this harder sequence:

A   Z   Y   B   X   W   C   V   U   D   T   S . . .

An inspection of this reveals a pattern. The sequential alphabet (A, B, C . . .) is embedded in the series, with two letters between each of the letters in normal sequence. What two letters are they? The first group is Z Y, the second X W. Does that make a pattern? It should, as they are the last four letters of the alphabet, reversed. To fit this pattern, the next two should be V U—and they are. You have solved the sequence, if you recognized the alphabet in reverse embedded in the forward alphabet. The next three letters will be E   R   Q.

Pictorial sequences are simple for some people but more difficult for those who cannot visualize. If you have trouble with visualization, and work better with words, there is an easy trick to help you see the relationships. Analyzing the sequence verbally will frequently give you the clue you need, even if you can't see it.

For example, in the following sequence, a visually minded person could see the direction in which the dots are moving. Someone who is not visual, or even a visual person who wanted to check, might verbalize the sequence.

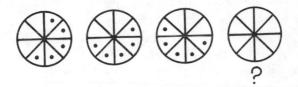

First, analyze the series, and describe it to yourself. You might say something like this: Here is a set of five dots in a circle. Each circle has eight sections. In the first picture, the dots run from the first section at the top right of the vertical midline to the first section at the bottom left of the midline. The next drawing shows that the dots proceed from the second section at the top right to the second section at the bottom left. In the third picture, the dots run from the first section below the horizontal midline at the right to the section just above the midline at the left. The dots, therefore, are moving clockwise, section by section. The fourth circle should continue the clockwise sequence.

Now see if you can either visualize or verbalize the following sequence of drawings. What should be drawn in the next picture?

The pattern has been alternating between an upturned mouth and a downturned mouth, and between upturned eyes and downturned eyes. Also, there should be a triangle right side up for the nose. The nose triangle has been alternating too, its point down where the mouth is downturned and vice versa. The fifth circle should repeat the first and third.

Similar to this idea is the idea of verbal analogies, which also appear on many intelligence and employment tests. Here, too, you must search for similarities. They may be overt, covert, or purely mechanical. The latter are frequently the hardest to find.

Take, for example, the analogy *loops* is to *spool* as *drawer* is to *contents/reward/bureau*. If you consider the relationship between loops and a spool, you may give your attention to the first and third alternatives. On the other hand, if you see that *loops* and *spool* are orthographic reversals of each other, you will pick *reward* without hesitation. That is a mechanical analogy, and does not consider the meanings of the words but purely their form.

In a more common type of analogy, the words bear a logical relationship to each other. Take, for example, *man* is to *mammal* as *lobster* is to *crustacean/fish/animal*. Obviously, it is *crustacean*, the class. Try *uncle* is to *nephew* as *mother* is to *grandmother/husband/daughter*. The key is older and younger relatives of the same sex, so the answer is *daughter*.

Try this one: *pipe* is to *rigidity* as *rubber* is to *hardness/ extensibility/flexibility.* Did you get *flexibility?* Rigidity is a comparable quality of pipe.

Your score on verbal analogies, incidentally, is affected not only by your ability to think logically but also by your vocabulary. If you don't know the definition of a word, you can't be sure of the correct analogy. So if you anticipate taking a test that will doubtless include analogies, study your vocabulary.

MORE LOGIC MADNESS

1.   There is a strange land, far, far away, where there are only two types of men, liars and truthtellers. The liars never tell the truth; and truthtellers, obviously, always do. You meet two men and, naturally, each of them is either a liar or a truthteller. You ask of number one, "Are you liars or truthtellers?" and he replies, "At least one of us is a liar." Now, using logic, can you tell: (a) Is the sentence true? (b) Is number one a liar or not? (c) Is number two a liar or not?

2.   A very simple logic problem can sometimes be apparently complicated. Without knowing the distances, or the times, you can logically answer the following question: Two airplanes set out from New York and Paris, respectively, at exactly the same second. Of course, one has tail winds, there is the rotation of the earth, and so on. Which one will be nearer to Paris when their paths cross in the sky (at a safe distance, of course)?

3.   You are back with the liars and the truthtellers again. This time, when you ask the question, man one says, "I am a liar but number two is a truthteller." Is this the same situation as question 1, above? If so, why, and if not, why not?

4.   The question that follows is a variant of a popular question, but it has an unusual twist. You may have seen a similar question before, but the twist in it should give you pause.

A princess on the island of liars and truthtellers married a man she thought was a stranger to the island. One day, along came a woman of the island and claimed him as her husband. He was charged with bigamy, a capital crime, and allowed to make only one statement in his defense. He said, "The person who committed big-amy was a liar." Did this help him?

5. Your child's toy block—a cube—measures two inches by two inches. What is the total area of all eight faces of the cube?

6. In a business presentation to a group of salesmen, the group manager says: "This new product was tried out in X territory. Our salesmen there were able to sell Y units per month. Most of this territory is just like the X territory. Therefore you should be able to sell Y units each." Set up a syllogism and point out either its accuracy or its flaws.

7. One parent to other parents: "Our son John is just as smart as Willie next door. Willie brought home all A's in arithmetic last month. Therefore John should bring home all A's in arithmetic also." Syllogism, please, as above.

8. "Everybody in our family has been successful. Therefore our daughter Susy will be successful." Set up a syllogism, or a diagram, or some form of logical arrangement, and argue from it.

ANSWERS

1.   Let us take this one very logically indeed. If the first man replies that at least one of them is a liar, then he is telling the truth or a lie. If it is a lie, then he is a liar, and hence the statement is not true, and both would have to be truthtellers. Now, you have just demonstrated that one is a liar, so that is obviously not possible. On the other hand, if the speaker was a truthteller, then the statement is true; he is a truthteller, and the other man is a liar, which makes the sentence correct, proving he is indeed telling the truth. By setting up hypothetical propositions, you can easily demonstrate this.

2.   This one has a trick to it. When the two planes pass each other, they are at the same spot. Therefore they are equally distant from Paris (or New York).

3.   No, it is not the same situation. No liar would say he was a liar, and if he did say so as part of a longer sentence (as in this case), the rest of the sentence must be false, since he is a liar. On the other hand, if he is a truthteller, there is no way in which he could say he was a liar, because it would be a lie. Therefore he is a liar—his sentence is false *for the second half,* or it wouldn't be a lie. Therefore they are both liars.

4.   His statement helps him because if he was a truthteller and the sentence was true, obviously he wasn't the bigamist. On the other hand, if he was telling a lie, then he was a liar, and the rest of the statement was a lie, and the bigamist was a truthteller, which he wasn't. Accepting his statement as true cleared him, because that made him a truthteller; and accepting the statement as false cleared him, because then he could not be a truthteller and the guilty man would have to be.

5.   There are only six faces on a cube! Analyze, analyze, analyze.

6.   Clearly, most is not all, and there is an expanse of territory that is not the same. Therefore the two areas are not identical, and this is an illogical conclusion.

7.   In this instance, the first statement—"Our son is just as smart as Willie"—may or may not be true. This is an instance where the logic is fine, but the initial premise may not be. Remember, if you start with a false premise, your answer may well be logical but untrue!

8.   This one can be worked out in a nice circle diagram or in a syllogism. It is very logical. The only problem is that "Everybody." Is it true? If not, then we can't tell about the syllogism. If so, then the statement is both logical and true. If you can point to even one exception to the first statement, it is false, and therefore the conclusion cannot be true.

8

CODES, CIPHERS, AND CRYPTOGRAMS

Shades of Mata Hari! Codes, ciphers and cryptograms have long had an allure that surpasses their actual value in everyday life. Somehow, for most of us, the idea of codes and ciphers is thrilling, steeped in mystery and redolent of beautiful ladies swathed in sables, of secret meetings on the *Orient Express,* and of glamour and romance.

Today, the reality is quite different. Cryptologists, working in this arcane science, have, for example, devised ciphers that are so difficult it would take even the fastest computers millions of years to solve. These particular ciphers belong to a class of mathematical problem known as nondeterministic-polynomial complete. But, by and large, code machines have removed the glamour from cryptography and turned the whole business into prosaic work. These are mechanical devices that simply have to be set up. The day of the single cryptographer, working alone in the dark of night to decipher a few words, has gone.

In this chapter you will learn how to crack codes and ciphers of every description—the old-fashioned way. Exposure to such secrets can sharpen your powers of playful thinking—a must for shrewd, inventive problem-solving—and enhance both your perceptual and your reasoning skills. You can also learn to be a master detective, knowing how and when to look for clues to seemingly inexplicable occurrences and tracing them to their logical solutions.

But first, let us clear up some common confusion about the difference between codes and ciphers. In a cipher, every letter of the message that is being transmitted is represented by another letter, a number or a symbol. If the original message is eighteen letters long, the cipher will also have eighteen symbols. We usually call this a cryptogram, and that is what we will focus on here. A code is different. In a code, a word, a letter, a number, or a symbol can stand for a whole phrase or sentence. A code book has a list of phrases or sentences, with corresponding numbers or letters or words, and all that is necessary is to transmit the identifying symbols. This sort of transmittal system has been used by businesses, as well as by spies, for many years. A set of code words was once used for cabling for hotel reservations, for example. In a code, unless you have the code book, you probably cannot decipher the message. Obviously, in a war, the danger of losing a code book is great. It has happened—often.

Since we are going to talk mostly about cryptogram ciphers, there are a few terms you should know. A *substitution* cipher is just what it says. Every letter of the original message has had something else—whether a letter, a number, or a symbol—inserted as a replacement. A *simple substitution* is one in which each letter is always replaced by the same letter, number, or symbol. This sometimes causes a problem: *e* is often a giveaway, since it is the most frequently used letter. Sometimes several different letters or symbols are used for the most frequent letters. (Just in case you are interested, the general frequency of letters in English runs: ETAOINSHRDLU, which you have probably seen.) A *key word* substitution is one in which the encoder uses a word, like "California," for example, and then places the letters of the alphabet under it. This is easier to show than to describe, so here it is:

C A L I F O R N I A B D E G H J K
A B C D E F G H — — I J K L M N O   and so on.

In this case, the word GO would be represented by R K. It would be necessary to work out the key word first, as it is not a simple substitution. (There are other variations of this, which are far more complicated.)

Another form is the *concealment* cipher. This is the type of message that hides another message. The point of this is to conceal the cipher so well that the message is not recognized as a cipher. This is the type that hides a message in an innocent-seeming regular letter, for example. Frequently, you must take the first letter of each word to form another word. An example would be a sentence that ran: Sally has insisted Peter Smith will . . ." That particular sentence, taking the first letter of each word, starts: SHIPS W . . . and could conclude with something like WILL SAIL AT SIX TOMORROW. Unless there was reason to suspect that a message was hidden in an innocuous letter or in a telephone conversation, it would go unnoticed. It is true that frequently such ciphers sound strained. It is often hard to work the first letters of words into a coherent message that does not seem slightly garbled, which would give it away to the censor.

One book on codes and ciphers relates that Sir John Trevanion was locked in Colchester Castle during the Cromwell period. In a message his friends sent, he read, as previously arranged, the third letter after every punctuation mark and discovered that there was a secret panel in his chapel, through which he escaped. This is one of the earliest recorded uses of such a cipher.

Another from the same time is the famous "pigpen" cipher, illustrated below. The lines indicate the position of the box in which the letter has been placed, and the dots indicate whether the letter is first, second, or third in the box. For example, GO in this cipher is ⌐ ⠿.

ABC	DEF	GHI
JKL	MNO	PQR
STU	VWX	YZ

Obviously, this type of cipher must be prearranged by the two parties using it. You can devise any shape you please, and any combinations of letters you choose, and as long as both of you have the shapes memorized (or a copy of the diagram), it will work quite effectively—provided, of course, you aren't up against even reasonably bright cryptanalysts.

There are many other examples of the substitution cryptogram. One that is sometimes used is a variant of the repeated code word. In this type, which you will find in many puzzle and game books, a code word is used and the alphabet is then put down, using all of the letters except those in the code word. Again, this is far easier to demonstrate than to describe, so here it is. For this rather simple form of cipher, it is important to select a word that has no repeated letters, as you must end up with twenty-six symbols. Take the code word BRAIN:

```
B R A I N C D E F G H J K L M O P Q S T U V W X Y Z
a b c d e f g h i j k l m n o p q r s t u v w x y z
```

The line of lowercase letters is the alphabet you will use for encoding your message. As always, E will appear more frequently in a long message than any other letter, but this method surpasses simply sliding the entire alphabet down one, two, or three letters, the very simplest form (in which A might equal B, B might equal C, and so on; once you get a clue, that code can be cracked instantly).

The use of the word BRAIN, for example, does scramble the letters, except for those at the very end. It is most certainly not a secure cipher, but it is fun, because if you can figure out what was going on in the mind of the cryptogram writer, you can guess the word, thus solving the problem instantly. If you can't, you may get some clues as to the code word once you have solved a few letters, and the solution then follows almost instantaneously—or at least as long as it takes you to write down the code word and the alphabet.

There is still one more method, of the thousands that exist, that deserves mention here. (This is not a history of codes or ciphers, and we have barely skimmed the surface.) The Vigenère table was developed by Blaise de Vigenère during the reign of Henry III in France. For centuries, it was considered to be unbreakable. All it requires is a code word, and an alphabet set up as follows:

```
  A B C D E F G H I J K L M N O P Q R S T U V W X Y Z
A a b c d e f g h i j k l m n o p q r s t u v w x y z
B b c d e f g h i j k l m n o p q r s t u v w x y z a
C c d e f g h i j k l m n o p q r s t u v w x y z a b
D d e f g h i j k l m n o p q r s t u v w x y z a b c
```

and so on, for all twenty-six letters. The chosen code word— say, ROSE—is then repeated over and over, above the message you are encoding:

```
    R   O   S   E   R   O   S   E
    a   c   a   b   i   s   c   o
```

The code would then require you to run down line R in the alphabetical chart until you intersected line A, finding the letter *r*. You would then run down O to the intersection of line C, which would give you *q*, and down S to A, giving *s*.

So you would encode the first three letters as RQS. The two a's are therefore represented by two different letters. Of course, it can also be done exactly in reverse, with the message on top and the code word underneath. There is no difference. Unless you have the code word, in which case decipherment is 100 percent sure and simple, it is an extremely hard cipher to break because the same letter may well be represented by many other letters. Frequency charts are of no value here.

Surprisingly, the French paid little attention to this effective cipher, but the Germans did. And it was not until Napoleon's time that real battlefield ciphers came into prominence, despite the availability of this very good method.

Ciphers had become so important by the time of the Dreyfus case that Captain Dreyfus was first condemned and then acquitted on the basis of improperly translated cipher messages.

AND NOW TO WORK

To test your wits here, you will have to decide what type of cipher was used, and then work on it. Don't forget the frequency distribution of English letters noted earlier. We have given some clues—you just have to spot them. Good luck and hppe uijoljoh.

The first cryptogram is a variant of the word square developed by one of the authors, and is called Terse Verse. The second line rhymes with the well-known first line, but is obviously not the completion of the standard rhyme.

There was an old woman who lived in a shoe:

   FB   JY   TMXAR   CL   UO   FII   IFVA   TDAQA   TLL

How to start on this? Let's look at it carefully. It does seem to be in word form, so it is probably a substitution cipher. There are doubled letters in two locations; that probably means the cipher is a simple substitution. If it had been set

up as anything else, like a Vigenère, the probability of two
sets of doubled letters would be much smaller. Since there
are two such sets in only nine words, each letter probably
stands for one letter. Try the frequency distribution first. There
are four recurrences of the letter A. Unless this was deliberately made complicated, there is a fairly good chance that A
stands for E. (Remember ETAOINSHRDLU.)

Fine. Let's fill in the Es. That would give us _ _ _ E _ and
_ _ _ E and _ _ E _ E. The most probable letters for the blank
between the two Es are R and S in a word this short. But let's
leave that for a while. The last word, of three letters, rhymes
with "shoe." It ends with two identical letters. Since it is an
"oo" sound, there is an excellent chance that it could be TOO.
If that is correct, you now have three letters, and can rule out
either of the two-letter words at the beginning as having either
an E, an O, or a T in them. That greatly limits what the two-
letter words could be. Place the T, which seems to stand for
itself, in the five-letter word on the first line. You now have
T _ _ E _ . You also have four two-letter words that cannot
begin with a T or an O, which should tell you something else.
Let's work on that T which stands for itself. If a code word
was used at the beginning, then perhaps the letters after T
also stand for themselves. If you try it out, you get the second
word as _ Y, and the last two-letter word as U _ . That gives
you an excellent clue. Almost the only two-letter word ending
in Y that makes sense is MY. Try it. UP is about the only two-
letter word making any sense that starts with U.

Now there is a glimmer of light. A = E, and Y = Y. That tells
you that most probably a five-letter code word was used, and
that the code word ends with an A. By this time, you should
be scribbling an alphabet based on a code word on your
scratch paper.

Naturally, given the title of the book, and the comments
earlier that you should try to figure out the mental processes

of the person making up the code, you have figured out that the code word is MENSA.

The entire cryptogram works out as follows:

> There was an old woman who lived in a shoe,
> IF MY TAXES GO UP I'LL LIVE THERE TOO.

There are all sorts of variants on these ciphers, of course. You can write the sentence backward; you can use numbers for letters, a very popular method, and you can also do what is done in many Mensa newsletters, and use symbols or figures. In the brief example below, the MENSA has been encoded in symbols. This will give you an idea of the way many Mensa members like to amuse themselves. The symbols are often clever little cartoon figures, or caricatures, for added enjoyment.

This has barely scratched the surface of ciphers, codes, cryptograms, and secret messages. We have touched lightly on a subject that has intrigued humankind for many years, and that is now more complex, more mechanical, and more difficult than ever.

CRYPTOGRAMS

Here are a few interesting and slightly unusual cryptograms that you might want to try. There are no ciphers or anything really difficult here. You just have to work at what you have just read.

1.   You should be in a reflective turn of mind for this one.

8 23 9 26 4 16 24 26 25   8 18   22 24 13 22 7 13 22 8
8 18 19 7

2.   This is a Terse Verse, based on "Jack be nimble, Jack be quick."
Finish the rhyme, which has been worked out in code:

22 10 7   14 11 9 10 22   10 3 21   5 10 3 16 9 7 6
3 16 6   22 10 7   20 17 3 6   11 21   21 14 11 5 13

3.   This one is slightly different.

    RGUA   IBW   UA   AKUFGRKT   SUDDWEWBR

4.   This is not really a cryptogram, although it is a variety of one.
Can you make the following groups of letters form a sensible sentence.
Hint: O?

FLME   NCES   HAME.   NYUF   LMET   WICE
SHAM   ENME

ANSWERS

1. This translates as: SDRAWKCAB SI ECNETNES SIHT,
   or, in other words, THIS SENTENCE IS BACKWARDS.
2. THE LIGHT HAS CHANGED AND THE ROAD IS SLICK.
   The alphabet used to write this message started with Y = 1, Z = 2, A = 3, B = 4, and so on.
3. In this one, the standard typewriter keyboard was used, but each letter was moved one to the left. For example, T = R, B = V, etc. THIS ONE IS SLIGHTLY DIFFERENT.
   (Of course you have figured out that it is really a substitution cryptogram, even if your keyboard is different!)
4. FOOL ME ONCE SHAME ON YOU, FOOL ME TWICE SHAME ON ME.
   All of the O's have been removed. (Removing vowels is a popular cryptographic device still, but it was used far more often several hundred years ago.)

9

HIGH-IQ TRIVIA

It is impossible to know just how many gifted children there are among us at any one time, much less, gifted adults wiring the electrical systems of their homes to a computer, dreaming up futuristic technology, or as in the case of one ten-year-old we know personally, connecting his adolescent sister's telephone to the stereo.

A popular figure, promulgated by the United States Office Of Education back in 1972, and doubtless as valid today, estimated about 2.5 million gifted children in the United States alone—to which is appended the warning that half of them go unidentified.

Misinformation has always abounded about the gifted, and indeed about IQ scores and intelligence in general. In this chapter we will help you sort facts from myths about high-IQ subjects and throw in some oddities, coincidences, and obscurata as well, strictly for your entertainment.

Are you tired of hearing about your friends' children's 180 or 200 IQs, for example? (And aren't we all?) Well, you should be, because unless those prodigies were tested back in the 1930s or before, they could not have made such scores. All standardized intelligence tests today have ceilings, which vary from test to test, but in the main do not exceed 166. And that is not to demean a 166 score, which is quite good, or your friend's child, who is probably a genius with knitting needles, or a prodigy on the bassoon. She just doesn't have a 200 IQ, on that you can make a bet. Perhaps your friend confused his child's IQ with her bowling score, or her blood pressure. This happens more than you'd think these days.

As you will also learn in this chapter, IQs in and of themselves mean very little, especially since most experts cannot even agree on an adequate definition of intelligence, and the tests vary, a score of 132 on one test being the equivalent of 148 on another. If you must hew to scores for measuring whatever you mean by intelligence, you'd do better to stick to percentiles—we'll explain why in the chapter.

And while we're at it, did you know that Winston Churchill failed the sixth form and finished last in his class at Harrow, or that Sir Isaac Newton dropped out of grammar school at fourteen, was sent back at nineteen because he read so much, and compiled an undistinguished record at Cambridge? Or that Beethoven's music teacher thought him a hopeless composer; and Darwin quit medical school? Consider that in our own time Nina Teresa Morishige was the youngest woman, at age eighteen, ever to win a Rhodes scholarship, and Merril Kenneth Wolf earned a B.A. in music from Yale at fourteen. The concert pianist Loren Hollander gave a piano recital for his classmates at the age of five, and was taken out behind the school after the recital and beaten up. Hollander likes to say that this was his first experience with critics.

It might also interest you that Elihu Yale reputedly left nothing to his eponymous university, and that Alfred Russell Wallace presented a paper jointly with one by Charles Darwin in 1858, based on his own theory of evolution, which was almost identical to Darwin's.

There are assorted myths about the high intelligence of ancient civilizations. One of the most famous of these stories has it that the Pyramids of Egypt are the products of a supreme level of mathematical and engineering achievement. Unfortunately, what they really show is the power of trial and error. Several pyramids fell down—the ruins still exist. The Egyptians tried several different sets of angles before they were able to compute accurately the angle of repose sufficient to allow the pyramids to stay up in the proper shape. There is one very squatty pyramid, obviously built by a pharaoh determined that his monument was going to stay up, no matter what.

Did you know that the famous artist Albrecht Dürer, known as a painter, a draftsman, and an engraver, is also credited with some major advances in geometry? Until the fourteenth century, perspective in drawings and paintings was not fully understood. (Just look at some paintings of that time to see the rather amusing evidence.) By the middle of the century, the "vanishing point" had been worked into pictures, and by the early fifteenth century, perspective as we know it had started to develop. Dürer made a special trip of over one hundred miles—a long, long journey in those days—to learn the basics of this "trick." He knew how to use perspective, but nobody had yet set down the rules in writing, or at least they were not published. In 1525, some three years before his death, Dürer's works on the theory of geometry and perspective were published. This book represents a giant step forward both in art and in geometry.

Another somewhat unappreciated genius, except perhaps by people in the field, is Hermann Ludwig Helmholtz. Though his training was as a physician, he formulated, mathematically, the law of conservation of energy. He also studied vortex motion in fluids, invented the ophthalmoscope, explained lens accommodation in the eye, and contributed to the sciences of thermodynamics and acoustics.

An unappreciated math genius was apparently the developer of ideas essential to computer programming. Unfortunately for Ada, Countess of Lovelace (the daughter of Lord Byron), women did not have much of a chance of achieving public recognition for scientific achievement. She did get a footnote in an encyclopedia and a 1985 biography.

Several men of high achievement, and probably geniuses, managed to kill themselves, in their enthusiasm to learn. Pliny the Elder (A.D. 23–79) was suffocated by hot gases from Mount Vesuvius. He was so enthralled watching the spectacle, and taking notes of this remarkable phenomenon that he did not remove himself to safety in time. We are indebted for the story to his nephew, Pliny the Younger, who may not have been as bright or as curious, but had more sense, as he removed himself to a safe distance and continued to record his impressions from there.

According to some sources, Francis Bacon, the Elizabethan philosopher and writer, also died as the result of intellectual curiosity. He is reported to have gone out in the snow in order to stuff the carcass of a chicken to see if the snow would delay the decay of the carcass. This seems to have given him a chill, which eventually killed him.

Other famous intellectuals have left us with eccentric bequests. One of the strangest was that of Jeremy Bentham, political theorist and the founder of the school of thought called Utilitarianism. When he died, in 1832, he willed his estate to University College, London, but only on condition that his body be preserved and brought to all board meetings. The Trustees followed his request exactly, and for about one hundred years, the mahogany and glass case containing his preserved body sat at the meetings.

In short, geniuses or not, we don't all use our intelligence to its fullest capacity at all times. On the other hand, there seems to be a touch of genius in almost everyone. Have you found yours yet?

Here are some of the facts of high-IQ trivia. Assuming that facts are the underpinnings of all knowledge, we do not delude ourselves that in the space of one short chapter we can give you the gift of knowledge, but we feel reasonably certain that we can contribute to it. And if we are lucky, you will enjoy yourself in the process.

1. Who gave his name to the first individually administered, age-based intelligence test, properly normed?
   a. Alfred Binet
   b. David Wechsler
   c. Napoleon Stanford

2. In general, what is average IQ considered to be?
   a. A perfect score on an IQ test.
   b. 100
   c. 150

3. F. Scott Fitzgerald is generally considered a literary genius of this century. What was his full name?
   a. Francis Xavier Scott Fitzgerald
   b. Francis Scott Key Fitzgerald
   c. Scott Fitzgerald; the F. was an affectation

4. The famed Wedgwood family, considered geniuses in the pottery and artistic line, also included somebody considered a genius in another field, totally different. Who was he?
   a. George Washington
   b. Isaak Walton
   c. Charles Darwin

5. What was unique about Louis Braille, who devised the Braille alphabet?
   a. He invented the first method of written communication for the blind
   b. He also invented sign language
   c. He was blind himself

6. Though Henry Ford is generally called a genius for inventing the assembly line, which revolutionized mechanical production, it was actually someone else's invention. Whose?
   a. Wilhelm Benz, of Mercedes-Benz
   b. George Packard
   c. Ransom E. Olds

7. All scores on IQ tests are comparable; that is, a score of 150 on one test presupposes a similar score on another. Yes or no?

   a.   No; it depends on the test

   b.   Yes; IQ numbers can be quoted with assurance

   c.   There really is no such thing as an IQ; it's just a convenient designation for a score on a particular test

8. Valid tests show that Leonardo da Vinci had an IQ of 150. Because of such tests, we can compare our intelligence to that of verified geniuses. Yes or no?

   a.   Yes; such tests are extremely useful for comparison purposes

   b.   No; IQ tests were not invented until the twentieth century

   c.   Not really; the scores you sometimes see are estimates based on the individual's early development

9. Geniuses burn themselves out at an early age by thinking too much. Yes or no?

   a.   Yes; most never achieve anything in later life

   b.   Yes; many have major difficulties because of their superior intelligence and simply fade away

   c.   No; they tend to do much better than average in adulthood

10. Genius can manifest itself at different ages for different types of high achievement and intelligence. Yes or no?

   a.   No; if you're bright, you show it early

   b.   Yes; genius in such fields as music and literature differs markedly from that in the hard sciences

   c.   Once a genius, always a genius

11. A true child genius described himself at an early age in these words: "I lisped in numbers, for the numbers came." Who was this?

   a.   John Stuart Mill

   b.   Alexander Pope

   c.   John Milton

12. Appointed a Concertmaster when he was fifteen or sixteen, this child played before Marie Antoinette and was considered by Haydn the greatest composer living at that time. Who was he?

   a.   Johann Sebastian Bach

b. Wolfgang Amadeus Mozart

c. Franz Gluck

13. This surprising military genius achieved notable successes on the battlefield while still in her teens. Untrained, she managed to defeat much larger armies under professional commanders. Who was she?

a. Mary, Queen of Scots

b. The queen of the Amazons

c. Joan of Arc

14. In what famous poem does this awed description of a lettered man occur? " 'Twas certain he could write, and cipher too . . . And still they gazed and still the wonder grew/That one small head could carry all he knew."

a. Homer, *Iliad*

b. Shakespeare, *Love's Labor's Lost*

c. Oliver Goldsmith, ''The Deserted Village''

15. Blaise Pascal, usually considered a genius in mathematics and philosophy, also is often credited with the invention of a remarkable device. What was it?

a. A primitive airplane

b. A primitive automobile

c. A workable adding machine

ANSWERS

1. (a) In the early part of the twentieth century, Alfred Binet was hired by the French government to develop tests that would distinguish between those who couldn't learn and those who wouldn't.

2. (b) 100 is considered an "average" IQ. It is the middle point, normally, on a distribution where 50 percent falls below and 50 percent is above.

3. (b) Francis Scott Key Fitzgerald.

4. (c) Charles Darwin was part of a very remarkable family, which included Josiah Wedgwood. (Note the spelling: Wedgwood is too often misspelled as Wedgewood.)

5. (c) Despite the fact that he was blind, Louis Braille invented the Braille alphabet of punched dots which is still in use today.

6. (c) Ransom E. Olds anticipated by several years Henry Ford's automated assembly line. Ford was a better publicist or had a better press agent. (Modesty did not deter Olds from using his initials for the REO car and his full name for the Oldsmobile.)

7. (a) and (c) The score on an IQ test depends on how the maker set up the test, and the numbers decided upon for what is called a standard deviation. That alters the shape of the familiar bell curve, and changes the numbers. For this reason, psychologists in general dislike the term IQ, and many testing companies have gone to euphemisms such as Academic Aptitude or Score of Cognition. Also, since tests cover slightly different areas, your score from test to test can vary; as can your score on the same test from day to day. (That's why percentile rank is more accurate. Your percentile ranks shows where you stand in an assumed group of 100. For example, if your percentile rank is 98, you are better than 98 out of 100 on the group that originally took the test, and on which the scoring system is based. Mensa accepts the 98th percentile, not an IQ score, for just this reason.)

8. (c) Since the IQ was only conceived within the last hundred years, all those stories about the IQs of various geniuses of the past are based on guesses and estimates. People have taken records of the early development of some of these people and matched them to current IQ tests for young children, and ob-

tained an estimated score. This method assumes that all of the information was recorded, that all of it was true, and that conditions were the same then as now.

9. (c) There are all sorts of records, chiefly the Terman study of the gifted, which show that very bright children do very much better than average in adult life. This study, done over a period of sixty years by trained researchers, found better physical and mental health, far higher achievement, and far more success in every sense of the word for children identified as gifted in the 1920s (the women did not, however, do as well as the men).

10. (b) The peak of achievement, and the continuation of such high achievement, differs markedly. In the hard sciences, achievement seems to peak early; in the arts and music, it seems to peak later and continue longer. Famous orchestra conductors are notably long-lived, and tend to continue their careers into what seem like incredibly old ages.

11. (b) Alexander Pope, in "Epistle to Dr. Arbuthnot."

12. (b) Mozart played before Marie Antoinette before she was queen.

13. (c) Joan of Arc achieved some highly improbable military successes.

14. (c) Goldsmith, in "The Deserted Village," speaks thus of the village schoolmaster.

15. (c) Pascal's adding machine was improved some thirty years later, in 1672, by Liebnitz.

10

THE PSYCHOPRACTICALITY
OF EVERYDAY LIFE

As you will recall—now that you have mastered the chapter
on memory—this is *The Mensa Think-Smart Book*. We mention the title again by way of pointing out that *thinking smart*
need not always be a function of higher intuition, or of sharp-
ened math or logical skills. Sometimes it's simply a new or
imaginative way of approaching everyday life, of solving the
practical problems we encounter in our homes or on the job.
It has been called common sense, horse sense, or even just
pragmatism. Without at least a modicum of this faculty, life
can become immeasurably more difficult (or just plain
annoying).

To be sure, we do not presume that with our advice you
will suddenly develop instant practical intelligence, but we
can show you clever ways others have approached specific
problems, and maybe some of their creativity will rub off on
you. At the very least, you will have a fresh solution to some
everyday problems that might otherwise have stymied you
when you came across them sooner or later.

For example, how do you know what time it is someplace
else in the world? If you are in New York and you want to
call Singapore, how do you know whether the person you
are calling is asleep, just rising for breakfast, or out to work?

There is a practical way to find out. In 1884, the idea of standard time came into being, along with a prime meridian from which all time could be measured throughout the world. Under this system, the globe was divided into twenty-four sections, each representing a certain number of hours, and the starting point, or prime meridian, was Greenwich, England, at 0 degrees. Thus, if you look at the convenient directory most telephone companies publish, you will see a plus or minus sign and a number (of hours) next to the name of each country on the list. This way you can figure out what time it is in the place you are calling. On standard time, for example, Greenwich is five hours *ahead* of New York (+5).

In this chapter we have gathered together some bright ideas and practical solutions to miscellaneous everyday problems that were sent to us by Mensa members. If you have any clever ideas and/or solutions yourself, don't hesitate to send them to us, care of the publisher. Maybe we will use them in a future edition.

One key to effective problem solving is ingenuity, or resourcefulness. An everyday example is the use of simple materials for a variety of purposes, especially as substitutes for the real McCoy, when necessary. We also refer to this as "lateral thinking". looking at objects designed for a particular use to serve some other function, totally different from the original.

The following is a prime example of such "handy" advice:

When I want to measure something small and don't have a ruler or tape measure around, I use my index finger. I know that each joint is 1 inch long, and from the fingertip to the knuckle is 3 inches. By marking a spot next to the knuckle and then moving my finger I can measure longer and/or wider objects.

For larger items such as tables, kitchen counters, cartons, etc., I spread my hand open so that the fingers and thumb are as widely separated as possible. I can now use the distance from the tip of my thumb to the tip of my pinkie, which is 9 inches, as a measuring instrument. If a desktop is 7 hand spans by 3 hand spans, that would translate to 63 by 27 inches.

A nifty "rule of thumb"!

Using the elements at hand rather than ready-made materials can often work wonders in emergencies. One below-freezing, blustery night, Mensan Morris Berwick of Kansas was awakened by the sound of his aluminum awning banging against the sides of his mobile home. The awning had been pried loose by the heavy winds. To fix it, he took a bath towel, soaked it in water, then ran outside and threw the towel against the break. The towel froze solid. "Fiberglass and resin could not have made a better patch," he says. "Two weeks later, when the temperature rose above freezing, the patch fell off. I then made a permanent repair."

Another resourceful Mensan resorted to brains, not brawn, with this one:

Two huge (6'5" and 6'6"), well-educated fellows (with five university degrees, including a Ph.D., between them) had struggled valiantly to open a dining table so that extra leaves could be inserted. They had already given up when I arrived at the scene. With my 145-pound frame, I knew I couldn't outmuscle them. But I asked for a 10-minute break, got the tire jack from my car and easily spread the two halves of the table.

The same writer reports that he has found "a hassle-free way to own a sailboat. In brief, I lease it to a sailing school. It is maintained by the school; I can use it whenever I want; they store it in winter. And they pay me rent. *And* I can depreciate it for tax purposes." Clever!

Still another artful way to cope is offered by this anonymous contributor:

For many years I've had an unlisted telephone number at no additional cost merely by listing myself in the directory first name first. That is, my name is David S. Stuart [not the real name, of course] and I'm listed under the D's (not the S's) in the Big City book. Curiously, no one has ever been able to figure out the system without a hint, though one Mensan managed it when challenged.

The only problem is the necessity of notifying the postal service that letters addressed to Stuart S. David are to be delivered to this address. And there's the added advantage of being able to filter out nuisance calls! Whoever phones and asks for "Mr. David" is promptly unmasked as a salesman. There's room for some harmless fun here.

Sometimes, perfecting the practical is a matter of sizing up your strengths and weaknesses—and protecting yourself against the latter. For example, if you are the absentminded type, you might have to take extra precautions, as in the example below:

I am forgetful and occasionally lock myself out of my car. My car is designed so that one key opens the door and works the ignition, while the other opens the trunk and the glove compartment. So I solved my problem this way: I put the trunk/glove compartment key on my house-key ring and I put a spare door/ignition key in the trunk. Now, when I lock myself out of the car, I use the trunk key to retrieve the door key. (This arrangement also means that I am not leaving my trunk/glove compartment key with parking attendants.)

At other times, the very best way to solve a problem is to *delegate* it. Knowing when something is someone else's responsibility will ensure maximum efficiency. One question on a final exam in a college business course asked: "How would you mail 5,000 advertisements?" The only student who answered the question correctly was the one who found the easy way out. Instead of quoting some tedious, easily forgotten postal regulation (an answer that was given only partial credit), the student responded that he would turn the matter over to the head of the mailroom, with instructions to let him know the fastest and most economical means of getting the mail out. ("On the test, I pointed that it was *his* job to know postal regulations, not mine!")

One thoughtful Mensan shared with us his general principle that "thinking smart" is merely adopting a new approach or perspective about a problem. "People who are not thoroughly trained in a given discipline and who therefore look at a problem outside the constraints of 'stereotyped' thinking are often the most successful at solving it," he says. Example:

You are no doubt acquainted with a game of blocks called Idiot Cubes. These have a mix of either four numbers or colors in different patterns. The object is to arrange the cubes so that all sides are the same number/color. This is usually accomplished by many (maddening!) trial-and-error turnings of the cubes until they match up. But the *nonstereotypical* approach is to stack the cubes and view them as a whole from above: A minimal movement of the head gives an almost simultaneous view of all four sides, expediting solution of the game!

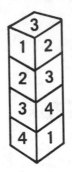

He sums up:

The two factors to "thinking smart" are (1) simplifying the problem, often by breaking it apart into elements, and (2) attempting to see the problem from a new or nonstereotypical viewpoint.

Another of his examples, especially for the visual-minded:

I find that I remember telephone numbers today more by patterns than by a series of numbers. For instance, 684-5135 is patterned so as to produce this mnemonic:

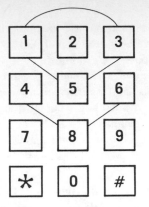

Still another Mensan, speaking generally, advises that laziness is efficiency.

Always ask yourself: Is there a better, faster, easier way to achieve a goal? Do I really have to run through steps A, B, C, and D, or can I skip one, or combine it with another?

Go back to children for clues on how to keep on learning. They are insatiably curious, always wanting to know "why?" Why does the dog walk differently from the cat? Why is the sky blue? Don't lose your sense of wonder—imitate them. Question everything. That includes finding out how things work and how seemingly complicated problems were solved. Approach knowledge with confidence. Know that you can learn anything you really "set your mind to."

EXERCISES

Try the following samples. In each case, think of a practical, lateral, nonstereotypical solution. Then check your answers with the ones given below.

1. What would you do if you needed taller poles for your clothesline and couldn't buy them at the time? (Your clothes are sagging on the ground and no amount of line tightening seems to work.)

2. You and your roommates have constant battles about who will get up to shut the windows in the middle of the night when it rains. The water pours straight in, despite screens and ventilators.

ANSWERS

1. Perry Oliver of Missouri simply lowered the ground between the poles by digging with a shovel—so the clothes ended up hanging higher above the ground.

2. In the second example, a certified original thinker (he later won a Nobel Prize in his field) cut the window cords, propped a stick in the window, and put a sugar cube under the stick. The rain or snow melted the sugar cube and down came both the stick and window. The stick, for more efficiency, was tied to something in the room.

Did you think of either of these solutions, or something close? If so, congratulations. If not, try again with one of your own problems, and see what kind of inventive solutions you can muster. This exercise is worth the effort, since it will encourage you to think in novel, original, "think-smart" ways.

Efficiency is yet another indispensable to "practical" success. June Roth, an energetic friend of ours, writes prodigiously (a total of thirty books so far, plus numerous articles) but still finds plenty of time for leisure because of her smartly organized filing system. She keeps thirty-one numbered manila folders, one for each day of the month. "The moment I receive an invitation to a business meeting or tickets to the theater, I insert them into the appropriately numbered file," she explains. "A meeting scheduled for August 10 will promptly go into the '10' file, etc. Every morning, as I begin my work, I simply look into the file coded for that day. I never jot down anything important on isolated slips of paper; it's always enclosed within one folder or another." Obviously, the same numbered system can be used month after month— no changes of file necessary!

This same efficiency expert reveals that she arranges another series of files for all her business trips, organized by city and date. Into every "trip" folder go her hotel, transportation, and other expense receipts, the reason for her visit, whom she conferred with, and what business might result.

"During tax time, this reference helps facilitate and document all my deductions for business purposes," she says. June also slips travel brochures in each of her dated city folders, should she ever want to return for a pleasure-only vacation.

One other suggestion: "If you conduct a great deal of business by phone, I recommend starting a 'scribble diary.' Mine is an $8\frac{1}{2}$ by 11 spiral notebook in which I informally take note of every work-related conversation I have throughout the day, recording the gist of the exchange—with whom I discuss a certain matter, what I accomplish, etc. Again, this is far better than jotting down the day's events, transactions, or important names on easily lost scraps of paper. Bound together in a single notebook, these assorted scribblings are useful when I'm trying to compile an acknowledgments list, for example, or send out greeting cards to business associates. I check over all the names in my book to make sure I haven't left anyone out. In fact, with this self-made directory I can trace back all the stages of any 'oral correspondence,' for whatever reason." June calls this idea her "junk drawer" backup system—an at-a-glance memory refresher that keeps track of how her work is progressing.

11

WHAT HAVE YOU LEARNED?

By this stage of the book, assuming you've been studying diligently, you should be thinking smarter. This means that your vocabulary is now substantially larger than it was before you read The Mensa Think-Smart Book, that you have increased your logical and mathematical abilities so as to be able to distinguish between the ouroboros and just any old gourmet, that your memory is now a retentive instrument in which you take pride, and that you can crack codes with such aplomb that the army cryptography corps as well as every ten-year-old is after you for help. Not only that, but in performing these various mental feats, you use precise and correct locutions at every turn. You are H. L. Mencken, Norbert Wiener, and W. V. Quine, wrapped into one. Best of all, you know who these people are.

Now stop for a moment and evaluate what you have learned. True, some of you probably already knew some of the material covered in *The Mensa Think-Smart Book*. That stands to reason, because you were smart to begin with, otherwise you never would have selected this book to read in the first place. Ignorant tends to remain ignorant. But you didn't know everything in the book, did you? And if you improved just your memory, for example, wasn't it worth the money? Or learned how to knock off one of those truthteller problems that have bothered you since you were at camp twenty years ago? Or finally learned how to use "lay" and "lie," correctly and easily? Or what a cipher is? Or some of the high IQ facts?

We'll see soon enough what you've learned and if you know how to take a test. Get through this final chapter and even you will believe you can think smart the way Mensans do. You might even want to consider joining Mensa, in which case we've provided information to help you, such as where to write for more information about Mensa (see page 124). Good luck on the test, and on thinking smart into the future.

WORD PUZZLES AND THINK-SMARTS

1. There are at least five common English words (and a few very uncommon ones) that can be made from the letters AERDC. How many can you find?

2. People have amused themselves for many years by making anagrammatic descriptions of famous individuals from the letters in their names. For example, Sir Walter Scott anagrams to "Last Scot Writer." There is an old and famous one on the name of Florence Nightingale. Can you come up with it? (Clue: It hints at her nickname.) Or with another one?

3. William Shakespeare. There are several anagrams that have been made of his name. See if you can come up with an original.

4. Can you solve this cryptogram?

   H O O L I   I V E V M   V M L G H   B H H L N   Z

   - - - - -   - - - - -   - - - - -   - - - - -   -

5. The following cipher will tax your wits.

   88-7-3-32-1-10-18-10-4-41-1-12-35-3-12-18-10-4-101-17-
   7-27-3-1-27-3-10-24-4-11-23-32-7-26-14-8

6. Memorize this list of names (use the techniques you have studied):
   Jim Wilson

Mary Jones

Ann Crackover

Reenee Lafallere

Joris Swinson

How long did it take you to make up a mnemonic, or a memory hook, for each name? Did you memorize all of them using some new method? Now put this list aside for a few hours, at least. When you return to the list, see if you can still remember the names in sequence. If you can, you have really learned them.

7. Try this list of numbers, memorizing them in the same manner.

794-2135

821-6006

967-3214

416-7865

423-6950

What tricks did you use to memorize the numbers? Could you make any words from them? Did you try to turn them into letters? Did you try to remember the numbers in sequence? Try to see which method was the most effective for *you*. Then practice that method. Do you find that you could remember a list of numbers more easily after this practice than you could before?

Keep a record of the time required to memorize five phone numbers: _____ . Now use your mnemonic devices, and see if you can memorize and recall five different numbers. Check yourself at the same point, and see if the devices you were taught (or taught yourself) reduce the time, and increase the efficiency. Time spent: _____ .

You should find an improvement. That's what you have learned to do—memorize significant material more effectively.

8. Test the logical conclusions in the statements that follow. They are typical advertising and political puffery and promises. Are they logical?

a.   The government of Anon City is corrupt and run mostly by corrupt officials. John Jones is a city official of Anon City. Therefore John Jones is corrupt.

b.   Home-baked bread pleases many people. If you bake bread from our mix you will please your family.

c.   Find the flaw in this conclusion: Every woman loves perfume. If you buy our perfume, the woman you choose to give it to will love it.

d.   Work out the syllogism buried in the excess verbiage and emotion of the family argument that follows, and point out what is correct or incorrect about it:

Spouse 1: We're overdrawn again and we still have some unpaid bills.

Spouse 2: Well, we had to buy that new frammis. The old one was worn out; the repairman said it couldn't be fixed, and we had to have it. The wiffler won't run without it, and the place won't run without the wiffler.

Spouse 1: I told you not to buy a wiffler—all wifflers have breakdowns in their frammises. This wiffler did too. You should have bought a service contract on the frammis, because all wifflers break down there.

Analyze this, put it into syllogism form, and then decide whether or not it is valid.

9.   What is the logical sequence of the following jumble?
A B C B C D C D E D E F ? ? ?
(Replace the question marks with the appropriate letters.)

10.   What is the logical sequence that these numbers are following?
3 9 7 13 11 17 15 21 ? ? ?
(What are the next three numbers?)

11. Choose box *a, b, c,* or *d* to complete the following visual sequence:

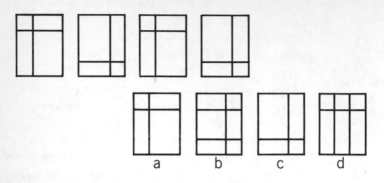

       a   b   c   d

12. *Plum* is to *grape* as ? is to ? (a) *Orange: lemon;* (b) *grape: vine;* (c) *prune: raisin;* (d) *peach: apple.*

13. *She* is to *hers* as: (a) *I: mine;* (b) *man: men;* (c) *it: it's;* (d) *you; ours.*

14. If you have two dice, one white, one red, and count each die separately, can you figure the probability that any one combination of spots will occur?

15. Without adding the following figures on paper, "guesstimate" the answers. Are the following series more or less than 100 when totaled?

   a.   8, 11, 9, 14, 10, 11, 10, 9, 11, 10
   b.   8, 7, 11, 10, 9, 10, 10, 10, 9, 12
   c.   6, 15, 15, 9, 9, 8, 10, 10, 10, 9

16. If you multiply two digits by 100, how many zeroes are you going to have in the results? Can you always tell?

17. If you multiply two digits by two digits, what is the least number of digits you can have in your answer?

18. If you multiply three digits by two digits, what is the least number of digits you can have in your answer?

19. Of course, by this time you have carefully reviewed the word analysis, and the making of new words. Now, to give you a chance to match wits and imagination with Mensa, here are a few fairly common situations for which no words yet exist. Can you make up a word, appropriate to each situation, that conveys the idea succinctly? Do your own, and then you might want to see what the authors came up with. (Ours may not be any better than yours, naturally. But see how ingenious you can be.)

a. The feelings aroused when your brother-in-law, who owed you $10,000 and doesn't seem to be in any mood to repay, drives up in his brand-new Mercedes: _____

b. The situation of inserting a most indiscreet or damaging letter in the wrong envelope and discovering it too late: _____

c. Making a fuss at your bank about an error on your bank statement and then discovering that you have failed to enter a check: _____

d. The sensation (for women only) of realizing that you have stood on a lecture platform for half an hour with a set of hair clips in plain view that you had forgotten to remove: _____

e. You discover you have worn one black shoe and one brown shoe to the office: _____

f. The act of forgetting the name of your live-in companion when trying to introduce him/her to your parents: _____

g. Finding that you have applied for your own job, which has been advertised (without your knowledge): _____

h. The problem of what to call your first wife's former husband's daughter who is considerably older than you: _____

i. The exact relationship to you of your stepson's live-in girlfriend's stepbrother _____

j.   The situation in which you discover that the employer who fired you is now sitting on the board of directors of the new firm to which you have just applied: _____

Surely there are words to describe each of these situations! And if there aren't, there should be. We are desperately in need of the exact word, *le mot juste*, for each of these complicated and complex parts of normal human existence. Can you find a good, one-word description? After you have written down your words, check the answers and see ours.

ANSWERS

1.   AERDC can make the common words CARED, CEDAR, RACED, ARCED, CADRE. (It also can make the less common words DACRE and ACRED; you may have found another.)

2.   A famous anagram for Florence Nightingale, is "Flit On, Cheering Angel." Did you find another?

3.   "William Shakespeare" can be anagrammed into several phrases. One that is sometimes quoted is "We Make All His Praise." There are several others.

4.   This cryptogram works out to: A MOSSY STONE NEVER ROLLS. As you found, the sentence runs from right to left, and the code used is the alphabet reversed: that is, Z = A, Y = B, etc.

5.   Have you solved it yet?

6. and 7.   To these questions on memorization, the answers are relative, of course. The important part of the answer is your own self-improvement.

8.   *a.*   No, this is not logical. If you set up a syllogism or a drawing, you will see that the word "mostly" is the equivalent of "some." Thus there is an area where "city official" and "corrupt" do not overlap, and Jones may be in this overlap.

b.   The same reasoning as in (*a*) applies here. The statement does not say that home-baked bread pleases everybody, only some people. Your family may not be among the some.

c.   The form of this syllogism can be worked out so that it is correct: Every woman loves perfume; this particular person is a woman; therefore she will love perfume. That does not make it true: Where is the evidence that every woman loves perfume? A logical premise based on an incorrect premise may be logical, but it is not necessarily true.

d.   The syllogism runs: All wifflers have breakdowns in their frammises; this is a wiffler; therefore it will have a breakdown in its frammis. Again, it is syllogistically correct, but possibly untrue. It would be necessary to demonstrate that all whifflers had breakdowns in their frammises before the argument could be true as well as logical.

9.   The alphabetical sequence runs three letters—i.e., A B C—then back one letter to start a new sequence— i.e., B C D.

Followed through for the length of the sequence, this would make the three missing letters E F G.

10.   In this number sequence, the pattern is add 6 (3 + 6, next number 9), then subtract 2 (9 − 2 = 7), and repeat the sequence. Followed through in that pattern, the missing numbers would be 19 25 23. Alternatively, take every other number (3, 7, 11, etc.) and add 4 to each to get the next number. Similarly with the numbers in between (9, 13, 17, etc.).

11.   *a.*   In each box the vertical line moves from one side to the other while the horizontal alternates between the top and the bottom of the box.

12.   *c.*   On the analogies, PLUM is to GRAPE as PRUNE is to RAISIN. A PLUM when dried is a PRUNE and a GRAPE when dried is a RAISIN. The analogy is between the fresh fruit and the dried.

13.   *a.*   A pronoun and its possessive form is the analogy. (One who mistakes "it's" for "its" could go wrong here.)

14.   The probability is one out of thirty-six. There are six possible sides for the first die, and for each of these there are six possible sides for the second. So there is one chance in thirty-six of a specific combination showing up; that is, provided you number each die and consider each die—the red or the white—as separate. This is not the usual way of figuring, but the question was specific about the probability of the two different dies.

15.   *a.*   This one is more than 100. You can observe that the amount by which all of the numbers are under 10 is only 4, while there is a 14, which would wipe out the difference, and several 11's.

b.   This one is less than 100. There are many more numbers under 10 than over it, so it cannot total 100.

c.   This will be over 100. If you check by inspection, you will see that the numbers under 10 are short of 10 by 9, while there are two number 15's, which will wipe out the difference.

16.   You have to have a minimum of two zeros. Of course, if you have multiplied by 10, or 50, or any number ending in zero, you will have more than two, but two is a minimum.

17.   You cannot have less than three.

18.   You cannot have less than four.

19.   These are the words that we think fit the situations. If you have come up with more appropriate ones, we'll enjoy hearing about them.

- a.   antiframobilism
- b.   embaragraphia
- c.   algorabarrassment
- d.   chevablusheria
- e.   chromoerrata (L.)
- f.   memorashamement
- g.   phobosalarius
- h.   Susan (or whatever her name is)
- i.   "Hi, there!"
- j.   ohorromus

12

SURPRISE!

NOT QUITE THE END

Last, but not least, for those of you who thought this book too easy, and elementary, we have included a surprise in Mensan code. Where it is and what it is are for you to find out. Solve the code, and reap the reward, or just let it go and wonder. . . . Still think it was too easy? Ta-ta.

The following twenty questions represent what you may encounter on an intelligence test, although we tried to make them a little more amusing than the average IQ-type question. Take the twenty questions and mark your answers carefully. Time yourself very carefully too, and work as quickly as you can.

Don't forget that Mensa has just celebrated its silver anniversary in the United States. Some of the questions reflect this theme, as they were specially developed for our twenty-fifth year.

1. The day before two days after the day before tomorrow is SATURDAY. What day is it today?

2. What comes next, most logically, in the following sequence?

S A I B L C V D E E R F A G N H N I I J V K E L
R M S N A O R

a) P Y b) B Q c) R R d) B R

3. What is one twentieth of one half of one tenth of 10,000?

4. What is the following scrambled word?

NNREAIVARYS

5. In the following examples, each set of symbols stands for a word. Study all three words given and the symbol equivalents and translate the 4th line into a word.

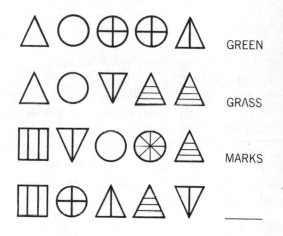

6. Which of the sentences given below means approximately the same as: BEAUTY IS ONLY SKIN DEEP
   a) Some actresses are so made up by the studios that you cannot tell what they really look like.
   b) Don't judge a book by its cover.
   c) Some people have prettier appearances than others.
   d) Good looks don't matter that much.

7. Which of the figures shown below the line of drawings best continues the sequence?

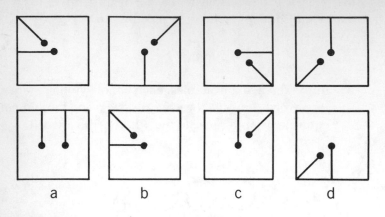

a   b   c   d

8. Canoe is to ocean liner as glider is to:
a) kite   b) airplane   c) balloon   d) car

9. Everyone at the Mensa party contest won prizes. Tom won more than Sally; Ann won less than Jane; Jane won less than Sally but more than Walter. Walter won fewer prizes than Ann. Who won the most prizes?

10. There is one five-letter word which can be inserted in each of the two blanks below. When you have put in the right word, you will have four new words, two on each line.

(Example: Place WORK on the line between HAND _____ PLACE, giving HANDWORK AND WORK-PLACE)

BOAT _____ WORK
DOG _____ HOLD

11. Tom, Jim, Peter, Susan and Jane all took the MENSA test. Jane scored higher than Tom, Jim scored lower than Peter but higher than Susan, and Peter scored lower than Tom. All of them are eligible to join Mensa, but who had the highest score?

12. If it were two hours later, it would be half as long until midnight as it would be if it were an hour later. What time is it now?

13. Pear is to apple as potato is to?

a) banana b) radish c) strawberry d) lettuce

14. Continue the following number series below with the group of numbers which best continues the series.

1 10 3 9 5 8 7 7 9 6 ? ?

a) 11 5 b) 10 5 c) 10 4 d) 11 6

15. Which of the following is least like the others?

a) poem b) novel c) painting d) statue e) flower

16. What is the following word when it is unscrambled?

H C P R A A T E U

17. What is the number that is one half of one quarter of one tenth of 400?

18. Which of the sentences given below means approximately the same as the proverb: "Don't count your chickens until they are hatched?"

a) Some eggs have double yolks so you can't really count eggs and chickens.

b) You can't walk around the henhouse to count the eggs because it will disturb the hens and they won't lay eggs.

c) It is not really sensible to rely on something that has not yet happened and may not ever happen.

d) Since eggs break so easily, you may not be accurate in your count of future chickens.

19. The SAME 4 letter word can be placed on the blank lines below to make two new words from each of those shown. Put in the correct 4 letter word to make 4 new words from those shown below. (Ex: HAND could be placed between **BACK** ————— **WORK** to make **BACKHAND** and **HANDWORK**).

HEAD ————— MARK
DREAM ————— FALL

20. Which of the figures shown below the line of drawings best completes the series?

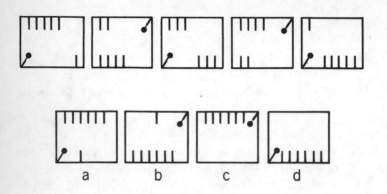

a   b   c   d

ANSWERS

1. Friday
2. a) The alternate letters starting with S spell SILVER ANNIV-ERSAR, and this sequence completes the phrase SILVER ANNIVER-SARY.
3. 25
4. ANNIVERSARY
5. MENSA
6. b)
7. b)
8. b)
9. TOM
10. HOUSE
11. JANE
12. 9 p.m.
13. b) both grow in the ground
14. a) alternate numbers go up by 2 and down by 1, starting with 1, and 10.
15. e) The only one that is not an artistic work made by man
16. PARACHUTE
17. 5
18. c)
19. LAND
20. c). The number of lines goes down opposite the stick, up on the side with the stick, and the stick alternates from lower left to top right.

Now that you have finished, here is how to interpret the scores, based on a limited sample of Mensa members who took these tests. Add 5 points if you finished in less than twenty minutes. Add 3 points if you finished in less than thirty minutes.

Total score 25: What are you waiting for? You're an excellent Mensa candidate.

Total score 20–24: You can almost surely pass the Mensa supervised test.

Total score 14–19: A very good candidate for Mensa.

Total score 10–13: A fair candidate.

If you would like to find out more about Mensa, write to Dept. SA, American Mensa Ltd., 2626 East 14th Street, Brooklyn, NY 11235. If you would like to check yourself on a standard IQ test, send $9.00 to Mensa for a test that you can take in the privacy of your own home, and that Mensa will score and return the results of to you. If you have not taken a paper-and-pencil test for many years, you will probably find this extremely helpful. If you already have scores at or above the 98th percentile on any standard supervised IQ test, write to Mensa to find out how you can be accepted on the basis of those scores. Mensa also accepts the SAT Aptitude section only, the LSAT, the GRE, the Miller Analogies test, and many other standardized tests. Good luck!

For information on Canadian Mensa, write to:

MENSA CANADA
Department TS
Box 505
Station S
Toronto M5M 4L8
Canada

or telephone: 416-497-7070.